14 Elements

of a Successful Safety and Health Program

■ ■ ■ ■ ■ ■ ■ ■ ■ ■ ■ ■ ■ ■

 **National Safety Council**

Acknowledgements

The National Safety Council thanks the following individuals for reviewing portions of this manual: Fred A. Manuele, President, Hazards, Limited; John H. Mitchell, M.D., Corporate Medical Director, AMOCO Corporation; Robert G. Petersen, Corporate Safety Director, ITW, Inc.; George Swartz, Director of Safety and Environmental Protection, Midas International Corporation.

■ ■ ■ ■ ■ ■ ■ ■ ■ ■ ■ ■ ■ ■

■ ■ ■ ■ ■ ■ ■ ■ ■ ■ ■ ■ ■

CONTENTS

■ ■ ■ ■ ■ ■ ■ ■ ■ ■ ■ ■ ■ ■

PREFACE

For more than 80 years, the National Safety Council has helped organizations address their safety and health needs. As a nongovernmental, not-for-profit, international public service organization, the council is dedicated to the reduction of preventable deaths, injuries and illnesses. Our mission "is to educate and influence society to adopt safety, health and environmental policies, practices and procedures that prevent and mitigate human suffering and economic losses arising from preventable causes."

In keeping with our mission, we present the *14 Elements of a Successful Safety & Health Program*. This manual serves as a framework for safety and health managers and others to use in setting up their own safety and health program or comparing their program to a model. This publication is a foundation and a starting point for building a safety and health orientation in today's global environment.

The Council offers a vast number of products and services that support each of the 14 Elements, including publications, educational and training programs, seminars and consulting services. Council programs and services cover employees in virtually every work environment and are focused on building an awareness and under-standing of the root causes of injuries and illnesses. Prevention is the key to a safe and healthful work environment. Our goal is to help you solve your safety and health problems. This publication is a first step toward meeting that goal.

We hope this information is helpful to you.

Gerard F. Scannell

Gerard F. Scannell
President
National Safety Council

■ ■ ■ ■ ■ ■ ■ ■ ■ ■ ■ ■ ■ ■

INTRODUCTION

Purpose of This Manual

The hallmark of the 1990s is a dramatic shift in the ways companies operate. Whether the key word in the company's halls is "downsizing," "right-sizing," "restructuring" or "reengineering," today's corporate managers are rethinking every aspect of their operations.

The goal of the National Safety Council in presenting this publication is to provide a management reference for executives and safety and health professionals to use in assessing their current safety and health programs and setting strategies for the years ahead. In this manual, we present the elements that constitute an effective safety and health program and the role they play in a comprehensive continuous improvement plan. A discussion of the application of the Continuous Improvement Model follows the description of the 14 Elements. A separate section ties continuous improvement into international applications.

The 14 Elements we address are the results of decades-long research conducted by the National Safety Council. In 1967, and again in 1992, the Council asked safety and health professionals for their views on the importance of various safety and health practices. The 14 Elements reflect the combined opinions of participants in the two studies.

Some similarities were seen in both studies. In particular, visible management commitment and involvement, together with solid supervisory support, in all aspects of safety and health program administration continue to be seen as critical factors in a successful safety and health management system. Differences between the studies were also apparent. A comparison of the study results reveals that today's safety and health professionals place greater importance on managing the human element within the safety and health system as opposed to engineering and procedural issues.

Successful companies realize that a well-run safety and health program is an integral part of a well-run organization. The 14 Elements presented in this manual constitute a recommended starting point for companies seeking to manage the safety and health process just as they manage quality and productivity.

Key Issues Facing Companies Today

Many issues drive companies today. For example, rapid technological change means that many products and services are obsolete sooner than ever. As competitors introduce products at a fast pace, individual companies are forced to accelerate research and development cycles. In addition to competition, other key issues that concern managers in the 1990s are product quality, productivity and operating costs.

Competition

In the past, companies faced competition primarily from other local organizations trying to compete for a small number of customers in a limited geographic area. Then, in the 1950s and 1960s, scores of companies began competing nationally. Today, a custom tool company in Muncie, Indiana, is as likely to be competing with firms from Germany, Brazil and Korea as it is with firms from Michigan and Ohio. The wide range of firms seeking market share in expanding global markets means companies must produce increasingly higher-quality products at ever lower costs.

Quality

Quality has been the clarion call for companies for more than a decade. Those that were able to adapt their products and services to the public's demand for better quality are surviving tough economic times. Companies that had allowed quality to slide, often by refusing to let the customer define it, have paid the price. Other companies have kept their quality focus, finding that the savings that come from less rework and fewer product recalls more than offset any increase in the costs of improved quality.

Productivity

Organizations are under pressure to produce more products and offer more services in a shorter amount of time. In a competitive global environment, meeting customers' needs quickly can often determine a company's market share and profitability. The challenge for companies is to reduce cycle time—the time needed to develop, produce and deliver goods or services—without diminishing quality.

Costs

The push for lower costs has led many companies to reduce the size of their work forces. The employees who remain often must do the same work, but with smaller budgets. The temptation to cut back in critical areas is strong, but safety cannot be allowed to become a victim of short-term thinking. Successful companies know that, like quality, safety doesn't cost, it pays.

Safety pays in two ways. First, eliminating preventable causes of injuries and illnesses can result in fewer disabling injuries, lower workers' compensation costs and lower replacement costs. Second, by eliminating or controlling exposure to hazards through an aggressive safety and health program, senior managers spend less time managing safety and health "crises" and can focus on all parts of operations, including quality, productivity and competitiveness.

The 14 Elements

The National Safety Council presents the following 14 Elements as the standard for a successful safety and health program. All effective programs contain these elements, but the emphasis on each will vary according to individual company needs. For example, a service organization might place less emphasis on some activities that receive top priority in a heavily regulated manufacturing company.

With each element, we present a review. The review is a list of questions or issues managers should consider when addressing the topics that constitute the element in their organizations.

Element 1: Hazard Recognition, Evaluation and Control

Establishing and maintaining safe and healthful conditions require identifying hazards, evaluating their potential effects, developing ways to eliminate or control them and planning action priorities. This process is the essence of successful safety and health management. We present numerous tools that safety and health professionals can use to recognize and evaluate hazards. Then, given the nature of the hazards identified, we discuss specific actions to control them.

Element 2: Workplace Design and Engineering

Safety and health issues are most easily and economically addressed when facilities, processes and equipment are being designed. Organizations must incorporate safety into workplace design, production processes and equipment selection. They also need to evaluate and modify or replace existing processes, equipment and facilities to make them safer. We explore how the design and function of the workplace can complement safety and health goals, minimize exposure to hazards and promote safe practices.

Element 3: Safety Performance Management

As in all areas of operations, standards must be set for safety performance. They should reflect applicable regulatory requirements, additional voluntary guidelines and best business practices. We describe how managers, supervisors and employees can be made responsible and held accountable for meeting standards within their control. We look at how job performance appraisals can reflect performance in safety and health, as well as in other areas.

Element 4: Regulatory Compliance Management

The Occupational Safety and Health Administration (OSHA), the Mine Safety and Health Administration (MSHA) and state safety and health agencies establish and enforce safety and health regulations. Other agencies, such as the Environmental Protection Agency, also issue and enforce regulations relating to safety and health in the United States. We discuss key aspects of international regulations in the European Union, Canada and Mexico. Staying informed about and complying with regulations are essential goals of safety and health programs. We also look briefly at conducting regulatory compliance inspections.

Element 5: Occupational Health

Occupational health programs range from the simple to the complex. At a minimum, such programs address the immediate needs of injured or ill employees by providing first aid and response to emergencies. More elaborate medical services may include medical surveillance programs and provision for an in-house medical capability. In addition, some companies are beginning to focus on off-the-job safety and health through employee wellness and similar programs.

Element 6: Information Collection

Safety and health activities, including inspections, record keeping, industrial hygiene surveys and other occupational health assessments, injury/illness/incident investigations and performance reviews, produce a large quantity of data. Safety and health professionals must collect and analyze this data. Small incidents often provide early warning of more serious safety or health problems. Complete and accurate records can be used to identify hazards, measure safety performance and improvement, and, through analyses, help identify patterns. The recording, analysis and communication of safety and health data are greatly simplified through the use of computers and commercially available software.

Element 7: Employee Involvement

Design and engineering controls are limited in their ability to reduce hazards. Companies now understand that their real assets are people, not machinery, and they also realize that employees must recognize their stake in a safe and healthful workplace. As employees become more involved in planning, implementation and improvement, they see the need for safer work practices. Solutions to safety and health problems often come from affected employees. We look at how employees can contribute to safety and health objectives through safety committees and teams.

Element 8: Motivation, Behavior, and Attitudes

Motivation aims at changing behavior and attitudes to create a safer, healthier workplace. This element describes two general approaches organizations use to motivate employees and stresses the role that visible management leadership plays in changing unsafe or unhealthy behaviors and attitudes. It also describes three motivational techniques: communications, incentives/awards/recognition and employee surveys.

Element 9: Training and Orientation

New and transferred employees must become familiar with company policies and procedures and learn how to perform their jobs safely and efficiently. The use of on-the-job, classroom and specialty training can contribute to a successful safety and health program. A complete program includes hazard recognition, regulatory compliance and prevention. The training is reinforced through regular follow-up with both new and veteran employees.

Element 10: Organizational Communications

Effective communication within the organization keeps employees informed about policies, procedures, goals and progress. We see how to spread the word about safety and health programs inside the company through the use of bulletin board notices, newsletters, meetings and other devices. Effective two-way communications between employees and managers is critical as is publicizing safety and health information in the community.

Element 11: Management and Control of External Exposures

Today's safety and health programs must address risks beyond the organization's walls. We describe the kinds of contingency plans and "what if" worst-case scenarios that are part of planning for disasters, contractor activities and product and other liability exposures.

Element 12: Environmental Management

Environmental management often requires a complete program of its own and is addressed in a separate volume, *7 Elements of a Successful Environmental Program*, available from the National Safety Council. Many companies, however, address environmental issues along with safety and health as part of their comprehensive programs. We discuss the minimum that an environmental program should cover, including compliance monitoring and contingency planning for emergencies. More aggressive environmental management incorporates pollution prevention and an active role in environmental improvement.

Element 13: Workplace Planning and Staffing

Safety and health considerations are important when planning for and staffing the company's work force. We consider issues such as work safety rules, employee assistance programs and requirements resulting from the Americans with Disabilities Act.

Element 14: Assessments, Audits, and Evaluations

Every organization needs tools to measure conditions, monitor compliance and assess progress. A variety of evaluative tools can be used to meet the needs of the organization, including self-assessments, third-party assessments and voluntary regulatory assessments. Numerous resources are available for conducting assessments, audits and evaluations, including the company's own trained internal staff, consultants and OSHA and other agencies.

The 14 Elements and the Continuous Improvement Model

The Continuous Improvement Model is a framework for safety presented in the National Safety Council's Agenda 2000® Safety Health Environment Program. (See Figure 1.) The 14 Elements are the materials that fit within the framework.

Continuous improvement is a process-oriented business approach that emphasizes the contributions people make to long-range, permanent solutions to problems. It is the cornerstone of total quality management.

Applying the process that forms the Continuous Improvement Model requires understanding causes before designing solutions. Improvements may be dramatic or incremental. In any event, the model helps ensure that they occur regularly. The 14 Elements presented in this book each provide a review to help managers focus more closely on the activities that each element encompasses.

FIGURE 1: THE CONTINUOUS IMPROVEMENT MODEL

■ Continuous Improvement Model

Phase 1
Management
Commitment &
Involvement

Phase 2
Establish a
Baseline
as is

Phase 3
Set Goals
should be

Phase 4
Implement
Strategies
close the gap

Phase 5
Review and
Adjust
could be

Safety, Health &
Environmental
Professional

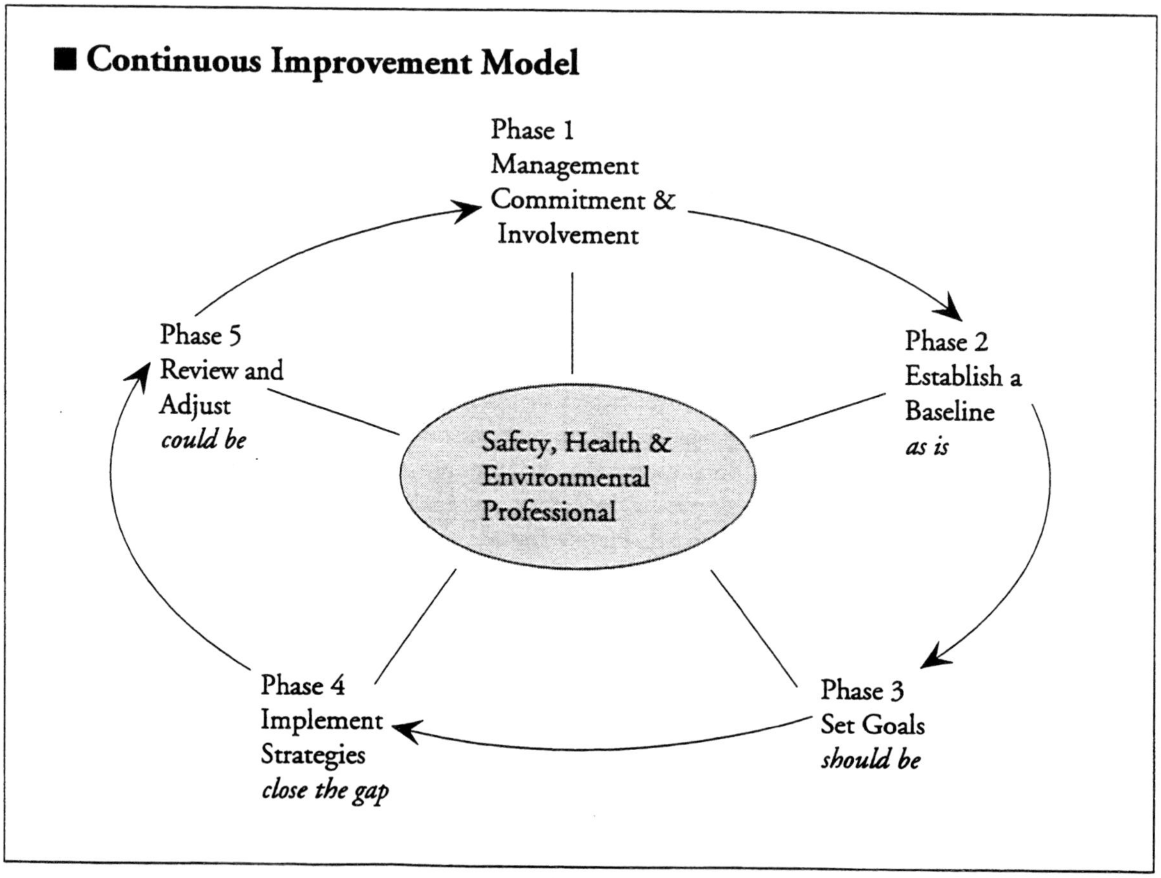

Phase 1: Management Commitment and Involvement

The first phase is to make a management commitment and to gain management's involvement. Companies with successful safety and health programs have active senior management participation. Without this active involvement, mid-level managers and front-line supervisors tend to ignore safety and health as an issue. Senior management signals its commitment by stating a position that is communicated through clear, unambiguous policy and implementation procedures. When management supports the 14 Elements, it also indicates a broad commitment to the issues included in the reviews. It then supports continuous improvement in safety and health through ongoing involvement, allocation of resources and feedback.

Phase 2: Establish a Baseline

The next phase in the Continuous Improvement Model is to assess the current situation by seeing where the organization currently stands in its safety and health program.

Teams made up of managers, supervisors and employees select an issue. The 14 Elements are an excellent resource for selecting issues. By using the review presented with each element, the team is better able to select an issue that is appropriate to its company's needs.

Once it selects an issue, the team takes a "snapshot" of operations relating to that issue. To learn what the "as is" conditions are, the team must first decide *how* to measure—review records (compliance logs, maintenance records, records of spills, training logs, waste manifests, purchasing records, etc.), observe conditions and interview employees for their experiences and opinions. Once these parameters are set, the team collects information and analyzes the results.

Phase 3: Set Goals

After the team establishes a baseline, the next step is to set improvement goals— what the operation or organization "should be." By setting goals together, the team ensures that buy-in occurs. What gets measured gets done, and the goals need to be measurable, to address the problem directly and to be aggressive. Improvement comes only by demanding results that can be measured. If they aren't aggressive or linked to a specific problem, people may not respond. For example, setting a goal to reach 100% compliance in wearing hearing protection is measurable, addresses the issue of hearing protection and is aggressive. Limit the number of goals to keep the improvement process focused and manageable.

Phase 4: Implement Strategies

Strategies are action plans to close the gap between the baseline (as is) and the goals (should be). They spell out what actions to take and who takes them, and provide a timetable for implementation. The team members make valuable contributions to designing strategies; they ensure that the strategy achieves the goal. During implementation, someone from the team follows up and monitors progress. Improvement is measured in terms of degree of goal achievement within the allotted time. Communication is critical; the results are shared with the other employees in the organization.

Phase 5: Review and Adjust

Results are reviewed and adjustments to the program are made to ensure continuous improvement. The key is to keep programs that work and improve or eliminate those that don't. (Of course, certain mandatory programs are always kept in place.) The organization begins to develop a vision of what "could be" in terms of safety and health. The process is repeated as the organization builds on successes and learns from less successful efforts.

Figure 2 details the steps that constitute the Continuous Improvement Model.

FIGURE 2: SUMMARY OF THE CONTINUOUS IMPROVEMENT MODEL

Phase 1	MANAGEMENT COMMITMENT AND INVOLVEMENT *vision and leadership*	■ Communicate a vision ■ Attend meetings and read reports ■ Set performance standards ■ Define roles and responsibilities ■ Be an activist
Phase 2	ESTABLISH A BASELINE *snapshot of "as is"*	■ Select a team ■ Team selects issues using 14 Elements and Reviews as guides ■ Identify key measurements ■ Conduct research ■ Analyze results ■ Communicate findings
Phase 3	SET GOALS *where we "should be"*	■ Add team members as necessary ■ Set goals ■ Communicate goals
Phase 4	IMPLEMENT STRATEGIES *close gap between "as is" and "should be"*	■ Develop plans and actions ■ Carry out plans ■ Monitor results ■ Acknowledge successes
Phase 5	REVIEW AND ADJUST *reach for where we "could be"*	■ Build on successes ■ Reexamine failures ■ Repeat the process ■ Communicate the process

Continuous Improvement and International Applications

Continuous improvement is key to voluntary international quality standards, such as those established by the International Organization for Standardization (the organization responsible for ISO 9000 quality standards).

ISO 9000 is an international quality standard adopted by the European Union (EU). Nearly all companies that want to do business in the EU will first have to be "registered" as complying with ISO 9000. The Continuous Improvement Model is consistent with the general procedure for registration. Briefly, these steps (as outlined in *Technical Communication, the Journal of the Society for Technical Communication*, Second Quarter, 1993) are:

1. Exhibit top management commitment to quality and have a strategic plan for quality.

2. Train all employees who contribute to quality and ensure that these employees have a hand in developing quality procedures.

3. Implement the new procedures and document them.

4. Conduct an internal audit of the company's quality system and fully document the results.

5. Arrange for official registration.

6. Respond and adjust to the audit as needed.

Another set of regulations affecting companies in EU countries is the EU Framework Directive. Its goal is to achieve "harmonization upwards," which requires all member nations to adopt the best aspects of the relevant health practices of each nation.

The effect can be dramatic. In 1993, the United Kingdom Health and Safety Executive (HSE) implemented six new regulations:

- Management of Health and Safety at Work
- The Workplace (Health Safety and Welfare)
- Provision and Use of Work Equipment
- Manual Handling Operations
- Personal Protective Equipment
- Display Screen Equipment

The recently ratified North American Free Trade Agreement (NAFTA) has heightened interest in how safety and health issues are addressed in the United States, Canada and Mexico.

According to a report issued by the Government Accounting Office, there are three major differences between the United States and Canada:

1. "The first is in who operates and funds the programs. Ensuring workplace safety and health is a federal responsibility in the United States; the provinces have this responsibility in Canada. Also, programs for preventing and compensating for work-related injuries and illnesses are linked in Canada but generally not in the United States. Employers in Canada directly fund health and safety programs, whereas the U.S. program is funded solely through a congressional appropriation.

2. "A second area of difference is in workers' involvement. In the United States, generally employers decide whether and to what extent workers participate in ensuring that the workplace is safe and healthy. Laws in the Canadian provinces mandate joint employer and worker responsibility and accountability.

3. "The third area of difference is enforcement. The United States and Canada differ in how occupational safety and health rules and regulations are enforced with respect to both sanctions and inspections. Penalties are used more frequently in the United States, while there is a greater enforcement presence and potential for immediate response to hazardous situations in Canada."

Differences also exist between the United States and Mexico. For example, in Mexico the federal government has complete responsibility for safety and health. State authorities only provide assistance in instances where an establishment is not under federal jurisdiction (i.e., construction and agriculture). In the United States, states can have their own enforcement under plans approved by the Secretary of Labor, in which case the federal government plays an oversight role.

The rights and responsibilities of employers and employees in Mexico and the United States have many similarities. One significant difference is that, unlike U.S. workers, Mexican workers can be fined for violating safety and health regulations.

In Mexico, ensuring safety and health in the workplace is largely the responsibility of worksite commissions made up of employees and management, who distribute safety and health information in the workplace and provide information based on surveys to labor inspectors and government agencies.

For more information on ISO standards, EU directives or safety, health and environment requirements for a particular country, refer to the resources listed in the Appendix.

Usage Notes

We avoid the word *accident* when referring to incidents that result in injury to people or damage to property. The word *accident* implies "unpredictable" and "unpreventable." In fact, most injuries are predictable (think of the last time you heard the phrase "an accident waiting to happen") and preventable. In this manual, we use the more accurate term preventable "incident."

The following chapters describe the *14 Elements of a Successful Safety and Health Program*. Reviews to be used when applying the Continuous Improvement Model accompany the description of each element, along with a list of information resources.

The reviews themselves lead the reader through a series of questions to ask when assessing how his or her organization currently addresses the topics discussed in each chapter. There are several ways organizations can use the reviews:

1. Mid-level managers can use the reviews to assess operations through a formal process such as the Continuous Improvement Model. They can assign a task force to complete the review for each of the elements.

2. Supervisors can use the reviews as a guide in safety and health meetings.

3. Safety and health managers can use the reviews when preparing reports and/or budget requests for top management.

4. Human resource managers and staff members can use the reviews when assessing training needs.

5. Senior management can use the reviews when assessing safety and health operations and budget requests.

The purpose of the 14 Elements and their companion reviews is to supplement an organization's ongoing safety and health program and to provide guidance to those who are just beginning certain aspects of their programs. The key point is *continuous improvement;* these materials are directed to helping companies in their continuing efforts to provide safer and healthier workplaces for their employees.

*E*XECUTIVE SUMMARY — ELEMENT 1

A successful safety and health program requires recognizing hazards early and addressing them effectively. Companies can use several tools to effectively recognize, evaluate and control hazards.

Management must first adopt a proactive approach to safety and health. Senior management's commitment and involvement are crucial factors in the success of a hazard identification, evaluation and control program. Management has a key role in communicating a safety and health-oriented vision, establishing policies and allocating resources.

Effective hazard identification requires evaluating all possible hazard sources, including management practices, equipment and materials, the physical work environment and employee attitudes and behavior. Several efficient tools are used in this multifaceted hazard recognition and evaluation approach. They include job safety analysis (JSA), safety inspections, injury/illness/incident investigations, industrial hygiene exposure assessments and systems safety reviews.

After hazards have been identified and prioritized, management must take the next step and implement measures to eliminate or control them. Methods for hazard control include engineering controls and redesign, administrative methods (such as preventive maintenance, housekeeping programs, hearing conservation programs, etc.) and personal protective equipment.

Element 1

HAZARD RECOGNITION, EVALUATION AND CONTROL

Effective hazard recognition, evaluation and control are central to a successful safety and health program. A hazard can be defined as any workplace condition, activity or feature that, by itself or combined with other variables, can result in an unplanned occurrence that can cause injury, illness or property damage.

Recognizing and evaluating hazards are ongoing tasks. Low incident and injury experience do not necessarily signify a hazard-free workplace. Safety and health managers must look beyond any temporary absence of injuries or incidents and adopt a proactive approach. The emphasis in this approach is on *prevention*.

Proactive hazard recognition, evaluation and control work well with the business management shift toward quality and continuous improvement. Effective management will produce work conditions and practices that result in job safety and health. A management system that focuses on total quality management through continuous improvement will address safety and health. Uncontrolled hazards signal a problem with the quality management system.

The cornerstone of continuous improvement is to strive for an error-free process. In safety and health terms, error-free translates to "incident-free," the goal of a quality-oriented hazard control program. Management must view the control of hazards as an operational strategy for improving productivity, as well as for assuring employee welfare.

1

There is no simple way to control hazards. Hazard control is the result of a continuous process that involves identification, evaluation, planning, implementation and reevaluation. It starts with the commitment and involvement of senior management. Management commits to effective hazard control through:

- adopting the philosophy and mission of working toward zero incidents
- endorsing the hazard control program
- setting forth written procedures to control hazards
- adhering to safe management practices
- allocating sufficient funds to implement an effective hazard-control program

Management's commitment to control hazards must be followed by implementation. Successful implementation can be achieved by:

- setting reachable goals
- developing and implementing strategies and procedures to recognize, evaluate, and control hazards
- periodically reevaluating the program's effectiveness

This chapter identifies the major tools used in hazard recognition, evaluation and control and describes how they can be applied in the continuous improvement process.

Hazard Recognition and Evaluation

Hazard recognition involves identifying the hazards in the workplace. Hazards may be present in any workplace and can be created by:

- management practices, including insufficient budget allocation, insufficient emphasis on safety and health issues, etc.
- equipment and materials used to perform the work
- environment—the physical, biological and chemical surroundings of the workers
- employees—people performing the work

Understanding the causes is as important as identifying the hazard itself. Hazards are identified through a variety of techniques, including job safety analysis, safety inspections, injury/illness/incident investigations, industrial hygiene exposure assessments, chemical process safety and system safety reviews. Each technique is used for a different purpose and under different conditions.

Job safety analysis

The workplace has many distinct tasks. Each task, from packing goods to word processing, has associated hazards. It is easier to recognize those hazards if each work task is broken down into steps and each step is evaluated.

Job safety analysis (JSA), also called job hazard analysis, is a systematic method of hazard recognition and evaluation. JSA considers each work task as a series of steps. Each step may have its own hazards. JSA identifies the hazards associated with each step, defines their potential hazards and identifies ways to eliminate or protect against them. JSAs are a series of written procedures that can be used by all involved persons to eliminate, minimize and protect against the hazards associated with particular jobs and their tasks.

The benefits of a written JSA include:

- standardizing work practices by identifying and specifying individual job-task steps

- establishing a framework for evaluating adherence to safe and efficient work practices

- creating hazard awareness by the continuing focus on prevention

- reducing the number of injuries, illnesses and incidents

- assisting in identifying causes of incidents that do occur

The first function in the JSA process is to identify the task. "Producing a machined part" is too broad a task for an effective JSA. A JSA task should be defined as a simple job or one activity of a process, such as "heat-treating the machined metal part."

The next function is to break down the task into steps. For example, typical heat-treating might involve the following steps:

- Transport the part to the heat-treating area.

- Remove the cover from the cooling bath.

- Melt the cyanide in the heat-treating vat.

- Transport the part to the cyanide vat.

- Dip the part in the melted cyanide.

- Remove the treated part from the cyanide.

- Transport the treated part to the cooling bath.

- Dip the treated part in the cooling bath.

- Remove the part and transport it to storage.

Although it is important to identify each discrete step in a task, it is also important to avoid task descriptions that are overly detailed. As a general rule of thumb, each task should contain no more than 15 steps.

After the task steps are identified, the JSA considers the hazards associated with each step. In the example above, dipping the part in the cyanide vat could result in employee exposure to the melted cyanide and burns from the hot metal parts. In addition, exposure to hydrogen cyanide gas could result when any plating acid residue on dipped parts reacts with the cyanide.

The final step of the JSA identifies the controls needed to minimize potential exposure. In the preceding example, the operation may have to be altered to:

- eliminate the hazard through redesign

- remove the employee from exposure (equipment or procedure changes)

- protect the employee against exposure (whole-body personal protective equipment, including respiratory protection)

A written record of the JSA should be maintained near the job-task location for easy reference. The completed JSA form makes it easy to track deviations from the established procedure. A sample JSA worksheet is shown in Figure 1-1.

Safety inspections

Inspections are conducted to identify unsafe practices, procedures and processes. Employees and supervisors should monitor their areas and equipment on an ongoing basis to identify and correct hazardous situations. If a hazard is observed, it is important to report the problem quickly and follow up with corrective action. A continuous, ongoing inspection program will aid in early identification and correction of hazardous conditions and may prevent serious injury or other loss.

Planned inspections at intervals provide a way to monitor the effectiveness of the physical aspects of the entire safety and health program. Inspections should be used in connection with other hazard identification and evaluation techniques.

There are several types of planned inspections, which may be conducted either on a scheduled basis or intermittently. The inspection techniques will depend on the type of industry and the specific situation. A separate written procedure should be developed for each type of inspection. For example, records, equipment and production process inspections may each require individual procedures.

Each written procedure should establish a timetable. The procedure should identify the job function of the individuals responsible for conducting the inspection, the subjects to be inspected, inspection format and guidelines for reporting, communication of results and follow-up. The written procedure also should include an inspection checklist and sample forms for reporting hazards.

Inspections are conducted by observing and comparing work practices with standard operating procedures, observing physical facilities and examining equipment,

FIGURE 1-1 JSA WORKSHEET

National Safety Council JOB SAFETY ANALYSIS	JOB TILE (and number if applicable): PAGE____ OF____ JSA NO.____		DATE:	☐ NEW ☐ REVISED
	TITLE OF PERSON WHO DOES JOB:	SUPERVISOR:	ANALYSIS BY:	
COMPANY/ORGANIZATION:	PLANT/LOCATION:	DEPARTMENT:	REVIEWED BY:	
REQUIRED AND/OR RECOMMENDED PERSONAL PROTECTIVE EQUIPMENT:			APPROVED	

SEQUENCE OF BASIC JOB STEPS	POTENTIAL HAZARDS	RECOMMENDED ACTION OR PROCEDURE

preventive maintenance and other records to ensure compliance. Inspections should be conducted by people who are experienced and trained in hazard identification. Inspectors may include safety, health or industrial hygiene personnel, managers, supervisors or line employees. All inspectors should be familiar with the processes and practices so they can identify hazards.

Generally, inspection frequency will depend on the potential for loss (i.e., property, casualty, business interruption, etc.). For example, a large manufacturing facility using hazardous raw materials will require more frequent and detailed inspections than a small business office. However, there may be other factors that dictate inspection frequencies, such as regulatory and insurance requirements.

Inspections can yield much information with respect to weaknesses and areas needing improvement. They are valuable in determining the direction of the hazard control program and in setting new program goals and strategies. It is crucial to implement corrective measures as soon as possible and follow up on the implementation process. Subsequent inspections will demonstrate the effectiveness of the follow-up.

Inspection results should be included in a formal report submitted to management. The report should cover the status of the hazard control program and areas needing improvement and should recommend corrective actions. Management is ultimately accountable for safety performance and must be involved in steps to improve that performance. Management also controls resources, and the inspection results may indicate a need for additional resources, such as more safety and health training programs, a larger staff, redesign of a process or the purchase of equipment.

Careful records of the inspection should be maintained. The baseline defined by the inspection will be used to measure improvement in the hazard control process. Written records are subject to the right of discovery in the event of litigation; therefore, they should present only facts, not suppositions or guesses. Reports should focus on determining facts and recommending actions.

Injury/illness/incident investigations

The goal of a proactive hazard control program is an incident-free workplace. In addition to a reduction in human suffering, low injury and illness rates mean higher productivity, lower insurance rates, and decreased workers' compensation costs. However, incidents can occur even with the best hazard controls in place. Although the primary objective of the safety and health program is to prevent incidents, a secondary objective should be to minimize the consequences of those that do occur.

All injuries, illnesses and incidents are preventable and are symptoms of problems in the safety management process. Investigations are conducted to learn the causes of injuries, illnesses and incidents so that they can be corrected and future occurrences due to the same causes can be eliminated. Investigations are an opportunity to learn and to improve the facility's safety and health program.

Investigations also increase awareness among management and workers of the importance of following established safe practices. The investigation should focus on identifying the direct and indirect causes of the incident. Indirect causes are the underlying factors (such as inadequate training) that, singly or in combination, lead to the direct cause of the incident. Investigations should never be used to assign blame. If operator error caused the problem, it is crucial to understand what caused the operator error. Was it a lack of training? Were the operating procedures clear? Was the job design at fault?

The nature of the investigation will depend on actual or potential for loss. All minor injuries and illnesses need to be reported, treated and investigated. Serious incidents require a more thorough investigation. These include incidents that resulted in or could have resulted in serious injuries, illnesses, serious property damage or business interruption.

Investigations of serious incidents should be conducted by a team that includes management, safety and health professionals and specialists in operating disciplines such as engineering, maintenance or production. Labor representatives and safety committee members (employees) may be involved unless otherwise controlled by an existing labor agreement. In many locations where a labor agreement may not be present, employers are opting to utilize employee representatives as part of a team activity. Under certain circumstances, it is wise to include an occupational physician or other specialist on the team. The team approach helps to ensure a thorough investigation. Conclusions and recommendations should be reported to senior management. Senior management is ultimately accountable and responsible for the safety and health of all employees. Investigation stages are summarized in Table 1-1.

Written procedures for conducting injury/illness/incident investigations should be developed. The procedures should specify when incidents require investigation and detail the process for conducting the investigation. The procedures should identify the investigation team members and processes for follow-up, reporting and communicating results. Management should approve the procedures, signaling support for and commitment to the program.

Industrial hygiene exposure assessments

Preventing hazardous chemical and physical agent exposures is one goal of industrial hygiene assessments. Industrial hygienists should be involved in purchasing new equipment and planning processes and facilities to prevent these exposures. However, some existing work environments expose employees to potentially harmful levels of substances or forms of energy. Overexposure to harmful substances or energy sources (noise, vibration, heat, cold, ionizing or nonionizing radiation, etc.) may cause injury or illness in employees. These injuries or illnesses may be observed shortly after exposure (acute effects) or only after a long period of exposure (chronic, or long-term, effects). When employees can be exposed to harmful substances or energy forms, it is crucial to determine exposure levels and to identify ways to reduce exposure. Industrial hygiene exposure assessments identify specific agents to which employees can be exposed and evaluate their possible impact on employee health. Exposure assessment results also are maintained for medical purposes as well as for compliance with regulatory requirements in the United States.

The assessment yields recommendations on ways to reduce or eliminate worker exposure. Industrial hygiene exposure assessments should be conducted by qualified, professional industrial hygienists. The assessments require special equipment and, often, complicated procedures to sample and measure the levels of substances in the work environment.

Industrial hygiene exposure assessments are conducted by gathering data on the nature of the chemicals used and on workplace levels of hazardous substances. The data can be gathered using several techniques, including personal, environmental, biological and medical monitoring and reviews of MSDS, process flows, etc. Data evaluation covers such factors as the level and duration of exposure and the toxicity of the substance. In the United States, OSHA has established standards for many of the most hazardous substances. The standards are called Permissible Exposure Limits (PELs), to which employees can be exposed on a daily basis.

TABLE 1 - 1. STAGES IN AN INVESTIGATION

Stage	Application
Identify and notify	After the incident, first provide appropriate emergency response. Address any injuries and secure the area to prevent another incident or destruction of evidence.
Investigate to collect data	Find out exactly what happened. Identify potential witnesses and interview everyone involved, including witnesses. If possible, start the investigation immediately. This is when details will be fresh in everyone's mind. Always stick to finding facts and not assigning blame. No one will be forthcoming with information if they think they will be blamed. Gather physical facts from the scene. An investigation kit including video and still cameras, measuring devices and other tools will be helpful for gathering physical evidence. The investigation area should be left untouched until the investigators have had a chance to observe, make notes and take photographs. Additional background information also may be required and can be gathered later. This may include a review of operating procedures, training and maintenance records.
Analyze data	Based on the information gathered, the investigation team should review the findings and identify the causes of the injury, illness or incident. Examine inspection and maintenance reports, incident reports and analysis results for patterns or trends. Causal factors to examine include management, equipment, environment and people.
Determine root causes	The root causes should be identified based on the data analysis in the previous step. The identified causes should be specifically stated. Causes such as "laziness," "sloppiness," "bad work habits" and "worker error" are inadequate. The conclusions must provide the groundwork for improving the situation. Generalities won't do that. A formal investigation report should be developed for each injury, illness or incident. Communicating results will increase safety and quality awareness among all employees. Providing management with investigation results and follow-up will provide the information needed to make policy decisions.
Take corrective action	The corrective measures must follow from the conclusions. For example, to address an incident caused by failing to exactly follow written procedures, corrective measures might include modifying a process to prevent "short-cuts," management reemphasizing safety and quality over quantity, retraining on the written procedures and training on the importance of safe practices. Completion dates should be established and adhered to. Failure to follow through on corrective measures can lead to criminal charges if the incident is repeated. All corrective actions require follow-up to ensure the corrective actions have effectively addressed the problem.

A workplace must adhere to these standards. For some of those substances, OSHA also has instituted "action levels"—the point at which employers must initiate some controls.

The American Conference of Governmental Industrial Hygienists (ACGIH) also publishes workplace guidelines for air contaminants. These are called Threshold Limit Values (TLVs). TLVs are updated periodically and provide guidelines for exposures. However, neither PELs nor TLVs are discrete dividing lines between healthful and unhealthful conditions. Exposure results need to be interpreted by an industrial hygienist who understands all the factors involved in the exposure.

Although many countries have adopted the ACGIH TLVs, these guidelines have been under review in some countries. The International Labour Office (ILO) in Geneva, Switzerland, periodically publishes a list of airborne toxic substance exposure limits for each country.

Exposure assessments can be performed at several stages. They can be used early to establish a baseline and repeated as the program is implemented and reevaluated. After completing the exposure assessment, a report outlining the findings should be prepared. The report should interpret the data, draw conclusions, and recommend specific actions to reduce or eliminate exposure. The best way to reduce or eliminate an exposure is to eliminate or control the emission at its source. If it is not possible to achieve a permissible exposure level by substituting a less toxic or nontoxic material, or by containing it at its source, then methods must be found to prevent overexposure through such means as exhaust ventilation or other engineering control, personal protective equipment or instituting administrative control programs that reduce exposure by limiting exposure time, for example.

Systems safety reviews

Work operations are often considered as a system of interdependent processes and parts. The system parts must interact in a specified way in order to accomplish the desired end product. Businesses commonly evaluate these operational systems to identify potential failures, inefficiencies or other potential production problems. The systems approach also can be applied to hazard identification, evaluation and control. By using the techniques described in this element, such as inspection and job safety analysis, it is possible to identify safety or health hazards, and the potential for exposure to the hazards, within the production system. Ideally, a systems safety review should be performed at the design or conceptual phase so the potential for hazards can be addressed before the system goes on-line.

After hazards are identified, they must be evaluated to determine their causes and their impact on workplace safety and health. Failure to identify the causes will result in failure to correct the hazard.

Unless a company has unlimited resources, hazards and their potential consequences must be prioritized so the most serious can be corrected first. Table 1-2 defines the types of hazards by severity.

TABLE 1 - 2. SEVERITY OF LOSS POTENTIAL

Severity of Loss	Explanation
Catastrophic	May cause death or result in loss of a facility
Critical	May cause severe injury, severe occupational illness or major property damage
Marginal	May cause minor injury or minor occupational illness, resulting in lost workdays or may cause minor property damage
Negligible	Probably would not affect personnel safety or health, but is a violation of specific criteria

Source: National Safety Council, *Accident Prevention Manual for Business & Industry: Administration & Programs*, 10th ed. Itasca IL: NSC, 1992.

A safety review should include rankings of hazards by their potential severity. For example, rankings for hazards might range from "very likely to occur within a short period of time" to "unlikely to occur." The review also should deal with the degree of exposure (relative proximity and duration) to the hazard; i.e., it should include an estimate of the number of employees who might be exposed and the potential exposure frequency.

Hazard Control

After they have been prioritized, the hazards must be corrected through implementation of appropriate controls. For each hazard, ask "What must be done to eliminate or control the hazard? Does equipment need to be refitted or replaced? Are better operating procedures needed? Is retraining required?" After the appropriate measures are identified, they must be implemented and reevaluated to determine their effectiveness in eliminating or controlling the hazard. Hazards can be controlled using a variety of tools.

Engineering controls and redesign

Engineering controls are implemented to eliminate hazards before they can affect employees or the community, making them the most effective way to reduce or eliminate exposure to hazards. Examples of the many engineering controls available include ventilation systems and process enclosures for toxic chemicals.

Some situations or conditions require redesign to effectively control hazards. In redesign, the system is improved to eliminate the hazard or exposure to the hazard. Because redesign may require rethinking the entire production environment, it involves the expertise of engineers, production personnel and safety and health professionals. In addition, redesign may entail a substantial commitment of resources that may require approval from senior management.

Redesign may be a costly process. It requires carefully analyzing the entire production process and replacing or retrofitting parts of the process that create the hazard. It sometimes requires redesigning the entire system to make it safer. Each facility must determine the costs and potential benefits of redesign in comparison to the alternatives. See Element 2 for a discussion of considerations for "designing in" safety and health.

Preventive maintenance

Preventive maintenance is usually thought of as a way to ensure that facilities, production equipment and processes continue to run efficiently. Preventive maintenance also can help to assure that hazards do not develop. Scheduled preventive maintenance should be a part of every facility operating procedure, whether that process is operating the photocopy machine or producing a pesticide. Written preventive maintenance procedures should establish a schedule for the maintenance, identify personnel who are responsible for the maintenance and describe a step-by-step process for keeping the equipment running safely. Preventive maintenance records should be kept and periodically reviewed to evaluate the effectiveness of the program. The records and procedures also should be reviewed during injury/illness/incident investigations to determine if adequate preventive maintenance might have helped to prevent the incident.

Personal protective equipment

Personal protective equipment (PPE) is any device, clothing or other item worn by a worker to prevent injury or illness. Depending on the hazard, the needed PPE may be used to protect the head, feet, hands, eyes, hearing or other parts or functions of the body. Appropriate PPE may include gloves, aprons, goggles and respirators, among other items. In most cases, PPE should be used only as an adjunct to other control measures. Effective PPE use depends on proper training. PPE must be properly selected, maintained and used if it is to control exposure to hazards. Some PPE, such as respiratory-protective equipment, requires special fitting, specialized training and a program that ensures appropriate use.

Hazard Recognition, Evaluation, and Control Review

Planning and implementing a hazard recognition, evaluation and control program is a huge and complicated task. It requires committing to a step-by-step process to make sure the program is comprehensive, effective and successful. The following worksheet suggests some questions and issues to consider in establishing or improving a hazard recognition, evaluation and control program. Review your company's existing program in light of these issues, questions and considerations.

TABLE 1 - 3. HAZARD RECOGNITION, EVALUATION, AND CONTROL REVIEW

| Issues/Questions | In Place | | | Action Plan |
	Yes	No	Partially	(if answer is "No" or "Partially")
1.1 Is there a written, formal policy to control work-place hazards? Is it up to date? Is it understood by all employees and managers? Are there ways to enforce adher-ence? Does the corporate mission statement address safety and health?				
1.2 Are there adequate resources for identifying and controlling hazards? Is there adequate staff and/or funding for inspections, JSA, PPE or to implement corrective measures as necessary?				
1.3 Does management communicate high safety and health expectations? How is this done? Has it been effective?				

TABLE 1 - 3. HAZARD RECOGNITION, EVALUATION, AND CONTROL REVIEW Continued

Issues/Questions	In Place Yes	No	Partially	Action Plan (if answer is "No" or "Partially")
1.4 Does management set a good example by following safety practices?				
1.5 In what ways? Is management involved in hazard control?				
1.6 Is accountability formalized? Are safety and health responsibilities formally assigned? Is there a structure? Who is responsible?				

TABLE 1 - 3. HAZARD RECOGNITION, EVALUATION, AND CONTROL REVIEW Continued

Issues/Questions	In Place Yes	No	Partially	Action Plan (if answer is "No" or "Partially")
1.7 Does senior management maintain involvement in safety and health issues? How?				
1.8 Are there written procedures for conducting hazard recognition, evaluation and control activities, such as inspections, injury/illness/ incident investigations, industrial hygiene programs, system safety reviews and preventive maintenance? Do they include assignment of responsibility?				

References

Books

International Labour Office. *Occupational Exposure Limits for Airborne Toxic Substances,* 3rd rev. ed., Occupational Safety and Health Series. Geneva, Switzerland: International Labour Office, 1987.

National Safety Council. *Accident Prevention Manual for Business & Industry: Administration & Programs,* 10th ed. Itasca, IL: NSC, 1992.

Articles

Ezell CW. Safety management: a new and better way? *Occupational Hazards,* October 1992.

Jones SE. The key issues of safety and health. *Occupational Hazards,* May 1991.

LaBar G. How to improve your accident investigations. *Occupational Hazards,* May 1990.

Lipman L. Safety and quality work together in the '90s. *Safety & Health,* May 1993.

Mays WM. Hitting the jackpot. *Beverage World,* January 1991.

Minter SG. Quality and safety: Unocal's winning combination. *Occupational Hazards,* October 1991.

Monough J. Accident investigation. *Rubber World,* January 1990.

Northgate EI. Auditing: a closed central loop. *Occupational Hazards,* May 1992.

Shapiro S. Global health, safety standards. *Business Insurance,* May 10, 1993.

Packaged Training Programs

National Safety Council. Agenda 2000® Safety Health Environment Program. Itasca, IL: NSC, 1992.

National Safety Council. Ergonomics: Awareness & Application. Itasca, IL: NSC, 1994.

National Safety Council. Job Safety Analysis: Identifying and Controlling Hazards and Managing the Process. Itasca, IL: NSC, 1994.

National Safety Council. Process Safety Management Assessment Kit. Itasca, IL: NSC, 1993.

Periodicals

CIS Abstracts (8 times a year). International Occupational Safety and Health Information Center, International Labour Office, 1211 Geneva 22, Switzerland.

Government Publications

State of California. *Developing a Workplace Safety and Health Program,* Document CS-1. Sacramento, CA: State of California, 1986.

*E*XECUTIVE SUMMARY — ELEMENT 2

Safety and health hazards are most effectively and economically addressed in the planning and design stage. Building safety and health into the workplace requires the involvement of safety and health professionals and others in planning facilities, processes, materials and equipment.

Safe workplace design reflects the optimum physical and psychological compatibility between the employee and the process, methods of operation, equipment, materials and machinery. A workplace designed and constructed with the employee in mind will have a favorable impact on productivity and quality, as well as safety and health.

A safe and healthful workplace is the result of a continuing process of design, evaluation and modification. Safety and health oversight on workplace design is essential to the elimination or control of hazards.

Workstations with automated processes help to make today's workplace operate more efficiently. But these innovative features may create new safety and health hazards at the contact points between employees and machines. Therefore, these contacts must be evaluated for hazards and addressed.

Element *2*

■ ■ ■ ■ ■ ■ ■ ■ ■ ■ ■ ■ ■

WORKPLACE DESIGN AND ENGINEERING

Designing "safety" into the workplace is as important as designing in efficiency. A workplace designed with safety and health considerations in mind will most likely enable employees to perform their tasks more efficiently, potentially resulting in higher productivity. Workplace features not designed with the safety and health of the employee in mind can cause employee fatigue, injuries or illness.

A safe and efficient work environment is achieved as a result of an ongoing process that includes design and various stages of evaluation and modification.

Safe workplace planning and design requires the involvement of professionals from various disciplines, including:

- engineering

- manufacturing

- quality

- maintenance

- purchasing

- architecture

- safety, health and environmental protection

In general, workplace design should take the following issues into account:

- the relationship between the worker and the job
- relevant safety and health regulations and standards
- facility, workstation, and machine design
- material selection
- proper material handling
- life safety and fire protection
- the safety and health aspects of automated processes

Safety and health professionals should be involved as consultants in the design stage, in start-up reviews and in evaluating equipment and materials proposed for purchase. Purchasing professionals must be aware of safety considerations and U.S. and international standards when making equipment purchases. Front-line employees also can make valuable contributions to the design process.

Design and Start-up Review

Although design and start-up reviews are two distinct tasks, their purposes coincide. Both tasks focus on ways to identify and eliminate hazards and minimize harm should an injury, illness or incident occur. In general, both design and start-up reviews are conducted to identify and protect against chemical, physical, biological, mechanical, electrical, psychological and ergonomic hazards before the facility, process or equipment is used. The content of the reviews will depend on the industry, on whether the subject is a system or a piece of equipment and on the nature of the facility. Operations or tasks should be segregated into steps as a more manageable way to identify the hazards associated with each. This technique, called job safety analysis (JSA), is discussed in Element 1.

Design and start-up reviews should evaluate the effect of the following factors on the safety and health of the employees involved:

- environment (chemical contaminants, heat/cold, humidity, lighting levels, noise, radiation)
- work flow (physical path, sequence, rate, duration)
- physical work layout and contents (size of space; type, size and location of instruments, controls and materials)
- work methods (physical and mental demands and information flow)
- guarding (physical means for preventing exposure to hazards)

Review personnel should evaluate each factor in light of the best technical information available, and then make recommendations to alter the design or specification to eliminate or control the associated hazards so that the risks are acceptable. Safety and health professionals coordinate input from other departments (purchasing and manufacturing, for example) to identify what changes are possible and which hazards cannot be eliminated. Hazards that cannot be eliminated through design are controlled through other means, such as placement and guarding of equipment to protect against exposure.

Ergonomic Factors

Ergonomics is the art and science of designing the work to fit the worker. Ergonomic reviews should be incorporated into any new facility design. An effective ergonomics program requires senior management commitment and continuing involvement to ensure that the program remains an important feature of the organization's safety and health policy and to guarantee adequate resources to identify, evaluate, and control existing and potential ergonomic problems. The ergonomic program should:

- encompass productivity, cost control, quality, maintainability and safety and health considerations

- identify existing and potential ergonomic problems

- recommend corrective measures

- implement improvements to enhance safety and health

- monitor the effectiveness of the measures taken

Ergonomic design addresses employee- and task-related factors so that the task can be performed efficiently and safely. The capability to perform a task may be affected by:

- an employee's physical condition, ability to judge, measure, reach, identify spatial relationships, withstand external exposures, adapt, etc.

- the tools used to perform the job

- the position the employee must assume to perform the task (is it awkward or static?)

- location (are objects awkward to reach?)

- strength requirements (amount, frequency, duration, muscles affected)

- the amount of force that must be used to perform the job

- weight of objects lifted

- frequency of motion (is the motion repetitive?)

- stability of the workstation (is the surface even and stable?)

A task that involves repetitive reaching for an object on a low shelf requires the employee to continuously alternate between bending over and returning to an upright position. Eventually, the repetitive motion of bending and straightening can cause muscle fatigue and eventual pain—signals of a mismatch between employee and task. Also, improper lifting techniques can impart sufficient stress on the back to cause a muscle strain or sprain. The situation calls for eliminating the need to bend by either moving the shelf, changing the placement of the object or altering the process needed to transfer the object.

Many injuries and illnesses related to hazards involving ergonomics become apparent only over time. Therefore, it is important to consider ergonomics in design review and job safety analyses (JSAs) as a means for preventing injuries and illness. Since hazards exist at the contact points between employee and task, the evaluation should focus on identifying the contacts and interactions between employees, equipment and processes. Then each contact point should be studied to identify the best way to accomplish the task efficiently *and* safely. Individuals involved in identification must be knowledgeable in research on human factors engineering and biomechanics.

One way of identifying hazards is by analyzing data on work-related injuries and illnesses (see Element 6 for a discussion of data collection and analysis methods). Also, by analyzing near-injuries or pre-illness conditions, such as fatigue, companies can identify hazards related to ergonomics before they cause injuries or illness.

These hazards are often signaled by a host of physical ailments. Some examples include:

- back pain
- wrist, elbow, and hand pain
- neck and shoulder pain
- blurred vision from eyestrain
- muscle soreness

The causes of these problems can be investigated using incident investigation techniques, except that participation is usually required from qualified medical personnel (see Element 1 for a discussion of injury/illness/incident investigations).

Codes and Standards

Facilities, processes and equipment should, at a minimum, meet all safety and health regulatory requirements. Many organizations also comply with voluntary standards established by public and private organizations, including:

- standards and specifications-setting organizations, such as the American National Standards Institute (ANSI), the National Institute for Occupational Safety and Health (NIOSH), the International Organization for Standardization (which established the ISO 9000 series of manufacturing quality standards), the American Conference of Government Industrial Hygienists (ACGIH) for chemical and physical agent exposures, and the National Fire Protection Association (NFPA)

- lists of approved or tested devices published by public agencies and private organizations, including Underwriters Laboratories (UL) and the National Institute for Occupational Safety and Health (NIOSH)

Many of the standards and guidelines established by ANSI and other organizations have been incorporated by reference into OSHA and other regulations, such as the Mine Safety and Health Administration (MSHA). In the absence of applicable codes and standards, organizations should become aware of and use the best business practice for the industry.

Safety and health standards are subject to change, both in the United States and internationally. It is important to stay informed about current and proposed standards or addenda to standards. Many European countries require adherence to European Union (EU) directives. The EU directives address such workplace safety and health issues as material handling, video display terminals, personal protective equipment and equipment usage. The United Kingdom has regulations in place to address these EU directives.

In Canada and Mexico, there is extensive legislation concerning safety and health. Companies should contact the safety and health office in the country or province of interest for the most current information. The best way to stay informed about standards, codes and best business practice is to subscribe to and read government publications (such as the *Federal Register* in the United States), as well as industry and safety and health publications. Please refer to the Appendix for sources of information outside the United States.

Machine Safeguarding

Machines with exposed moving parts can easily cause serious injury. Critical design features include those that prevent employees from coming into contact with the moving parts, eliminate or guard cutting edges and nip points, eliminate hot areas, etc., so that injury can be avoided. Whenever possible, companies should incorporate safeguarding into the design of machines. When a new piece of equipment is being considered or planned, the safety and health professional should evaluate the hazards posed by the machine. He or she should consider how the machine will be used, who will use it, how often it will be used and why. Using job safety analysis (JSA, see Element 1), the professional should evaluate each step in the machine's operation to identify all possible operator contacts with machine hazards.

There are numerous ways to safeguard machines. These safeguards will depend on the use of the machine and the possible hazard. Machine safeguarding types include:

- physical barriers
- electronic barriers
- electrical interlocks
- mechanical pull-back and sweep devices
- guarding by location

Machine safeguards can be designed or built in or, if necessary, added later.

Material Handling

Within every business, there are material handling needs. Industrial operations, for example, must move raw material, component parts and finished products within the facility. Material handling is one of the most common tasks performed in an industrial setting.

Material handling accounts for 28% of all occupational injuries. If the materials are handled manually (without mechanical, hydraulic or other automated materials handling equipment), there are ergonomic hazards associated with lifting, carrying and placing. The National Institute for Occupational Safety and Health (NIOSH) has published lifting guidelines (for further information, see References).

Designers of systems and procedures should consider alternative ways for handling materials that will eliminate or minimize worker contact through, for example, automation or manually controlled assists.

Procedures for handling all materials, whether manually or by automated means, must be reviewed to identify hazards. Examples of material handling hazards include:

- sharp edges
- acids or other toxic or hazardous substances packed in breakable containers
- irritating dust
- excessive load movement
- load weight and stability
- transport difference and elevation change
- load manipulation

Ways to eliminate or control hazards should be defined, prioritized and implemented; for example:

- substitute materials
- use handling aids
- automate processes
- decrease load weight
- provide additional training

Automated Processes

Automated processes can save time, money and effort. While they minimize exposure to the hazards of the process, they can also create a new set of hazards to which employees can be exposed during operation, maintenance, equipment adjustments, sampling, etc. These exposures must be addressed.

The nature of automated process hazards varies depending on the industry, the complexity and size of the systems, etc. The safety and health professional, along with an engineer who understands robotics, must thoroughly evaluate the process, identify all potential failure modes and contact points between humans and the process and define all hazards. The design of the process should, if possible, eliminate hazards, minimize exposure to hazards and control the results of process failures. After the system is in place, and before it is on-line, the safety and health professional should evaluate the system again to identify any additional hazards undetected during design, construction and installation. These additional hazards should be addressed before the system is brought into operation.

Life Safety and Fire Protection

Adequate fire protection and life safety controls can minimize loss of life and property. Workplace design and construction are critical to fire protection and life safety. According to the National Fire Protection Association (NFPA), fire protection measures should have the following general objectives:

- saving lives
- continuing operations
- protecting property

Workplace design should address each of these objectives. To accomplish this, the designer must understand the uses and functions of the facility.

Whether the facility is in the planning stage or already constructed, safety and health professionals should identify fire hazards and recommend ways to eliminate them or minimize the potential consequences of a fire or explosion. This process is called a fire hazard analysis. The issues considered in fire hazard analysis include:

- site (location, accessibility, age)
- construction materials and design
- contents
- operations
- management of the facility
- people (who is using the facility, and how)
- fire protection system (detection, alarms, communication, automatic sprinklers, portable fire extinguishers, fire brigades)
- emergency plans/procedures/evacuation

Effective fire protection measures are a function of the use made of the facility, the people in the facility and their actions, the potential for loss and the magnitude of existing hazards.

Additionally, specific fire codes must be followed as a minimum (both construction and performance codes). A facility's design should include:

- fire-resistant construction with fire divisions and self-closing fire doors
- easy access to and exit from the facility interior
- a fire detection and alarm system
- an automatic sprinkler system
- ready access to the facility to minimize emergency response time
- adequate water supply
- adequate portable fire extinguishers and other fire-fighting equipment
- appropriate specialty equipment common to certain industries, such as blowout panels where explosions are possible, fixed nonwater fire-suppression systems for valuable material storage areas (computer rooms, records storage and other important document repositories, etc.)

Formal procedures for checking, testing and maintaining fire-protection equipment should be established and understood by employees who are assigned these responsibilities. The procedures identify responsible individuals and schedules and provide a means to monitor adherence. Procedures and equipment should be reviewed on an ongoing basis to identify needs and potential problems.

Workplace Design and Engineering Review

Safety and health needs to be an integral part of workplace design considerations. As a start, safety and health professionals and others should evaluate how safety and health considerations are currently incorporated into workplace design and engineering decisions. Then, they need to consider where there are gaps and problems, define and implement actions and, finally, reevaluate. The following review suggests some questions and issues to be addressed when evaluating existing workplace design and engineering program activities.

TABLE 2 - 1. WORKPLACE DESIGN AND ENGINEERING REVIEW

| Issues/Questions | In Place | | | Action Plan |
	Yes	No	Partially	(if answer is "No" or "Partially")
2.1 Does management understand and adopt an "up-front" and "design in" approach to engineering and design?				
2.2 Does management communicate high priority for built-in safety?				
2.3 Does management place a high priority on process safety management for any automated processes?				
2.4 Does the organization have a policy to adhere to all relevant codes and standards, voluntary and statutory?				
2.5 Is a procedure in place for conducting pre-design and pre-start-up reviews?				
2.6 Is adequate funding available for necessary analyses and reporting?				
2.7 Are those responsible for design trained in hazard identification and evaluation techniques?				

TABLE 2 - 1. WORKPLACE DESIGN AND ENGINEERING REVIEW Continued

Issues/Questions	In Place Yes	No	Partially	Action Plan (if answer is "No" or "Partially")
2.8 Are safety and health recommendations taken seriously and addressed in design?				
2.9 Are safety and health professionals involved in design and engineering decisions?				
2.10 Does management have a formal fire safety policy, with saving lives as the primary objective?				
2.11 Are reviews conducted always? sometimes? occasionally? never?				
2.12 Is the review procedure complete and adequate?				
2.13 Are ergonomic consid- erations regularly addressed in design and purchasing decisions?				
2.14 Are copies of all appli- cable codes and standards on-site and reviewed?				

TABLE 2 - 1. WORKPLACE DESIGN AND ENGINEERING REVIEW Continued

| Issues/Questions | In Place | | | Action Plan |
	Yes	No	Partially	(if answer is "No" or "Partially")
2.15 Have facilities and processes been evaluated for adherence to codes and standards?				
2.16 Is a procedure in place for monitoring code adherence on a continuing basis?				
2.17 Does the safety and health department provide input into facility, workstation, and machine design specifications?				
2.18 Do procedures exist for fire safety analysis?				
2.19 Is fire safety analysis performed regularly?				
2.20 Are hazards involving material handling evaluation procedures in place?				
2.21 Is evaluation of material handling procedures performed on an adequate schedule?				

References

Books

Brauer RL. *Safety and Health for Engineers*. New York: Van Nostrand Reinhold, 1990.

Bugbee P. *Principles of Fire Protection*. Quincy, MA: National Fire Protection Association, 1990.

Manuele F. *On the Practice of Safety*. New York: Van Nostrand Reinhold, 1993.

National Safety Council. *Accident Prevention Manual for Business & Industry: Engineering & Technology*, 10th ed. Itasca, IL: NSC, 1992.

Stephenson J. *System Safety 2000*. New York: Van Nostrand Reinhold, 1991.

Articles

Christenson JA. The essence of hazard control. *Risk Management*, June 1992.

Fidderman H. State of play table. *Eurosafety* (England), Winter 1993.

Hockman K, Erdman A. Gearing up for ISO 9000 registration. *Chemical Engineering*, April 1993.

Katzel J. Introduction to ergonomics. *Plant Engineering*, June 6, 1991.

Kertesz L. Human machines need good workplace design. *Business Insurance*, April 13, 1992.

Kittusamy NK, et al. A preliminary audit for ergonomics design in manufacturing environments. *Industrial Engineering*, July 1992.

Minter SG. Avoiding the big bang. *Occupational Hazards*, July 1990.

Vasilash GS. Designing better places to work. *Production*, February 1990.

Waters TR, Putz-Anderson V, Garg A, Fine LJ. Revised NIOSH equation for the design and evaluation of manual lifting tasks. *Ergonomics*, vol. 36, no. 7, July 1993.

Packaged Training Program

National Safety Council. Agenda 2000® Safety Health Environment Program. Itasca, IL: NSC, 1992.

EXECUTIVE SUMMARY — ELEMENT 3

Even a work environment designed for safety and health will not prevent injuries and illness unless people perform their tasks safely. Successful safety management must address performance. Companies committed to safety and health will examine the factors that affect performance and the tools used to measure and improve it.

Successful safety and health performance is possible when the organization has a clear, well-communicated, performance-oriented vision for safety and health. The vision must come from senior management and must be carried out by safety and health professionals, managers and employees, with senior management involvement throughout the process.

The key to high quality and consistent safety and health performance is adhering to a set of established standards and guidelines. These standards can be set from within an organization, imposed by external sources (such as regulatory authorities) or adopted from an external source (such as a standards-setting organization). Holding individuals accountable for adhering to standards emphasizes the importance of and helps to ensure safe performance.

Monitoring performance through performance reviews and appraisals can help management identify problems and solutions. Performance reviews use numerical performance data to evaluate compliance with safety performance standards and to communicate the findings to senior management.

■ ■ ■ ■ ■ ■ ■ ■ ■ ■ ■ ■ ■ ■

SAFETY PERFORMANCE MANAGEMENT

Effective safety and health management operates on two levels. The first level is the physical work environment: facilities, materials and equipment. Addressing safety and health on this level focuses on safe design and engineering. But even the most effectively designed work environment will not prevent injuries and illnesses unless people perform their tasks properly. Therefore, successful safety management must also address safety and health on the second level: performance—the actions of employees in relation to the work environment.

Successful safety performance is possible when the organization has a clear and well-communicated vision for safety and health that is supported by reachable goals. The company must establish standards for safe work practices and develop procedures to conform with the standards. Conformance with standards depends on effective communication so that employees at all levels understand and comply with expectations and requirements.

Roles and Responsibilities in Safety Performance

Successful safety performance management is an ongoing and continuous process involving all levels of management and employees, each with responsibilities, roles and accountability.

Senior management establishes company policy and is ultimately responsible for the safety and health of the company's employees. Successful safety performance depends on the continuing involvement, interest and financial support of senior management.

Management's attitude toward safety and health tends to be reflected throughout the organization; therefore, senior managers must acknowledge that a safe workplace makes good business sense. Table 3-1 identifies safety and health considerations with respect to business issues.

TABLE 3 - 1. SAFETY AND HEALTH CONSIDERATIONS IN BUSINESS

Business issue	Safety and health considerations
Financial	Consider the short- and long-term costs of adopting effective safety and health standards versus the increased cost of workers' compensation claims, lost time and other direct and indirect costs associated with a less effective program.
Regulatory/legal	Regulatory agencies aggressively enforce regulations; they can impose fines and cause operations interruptions. Companies and individuals may be held criminally liable for violations. The cost of litigating citations and proposed penalties against the company should also be considered. If found in violation, the company can lose some flexibility in how it allocates its resources. For uncontested violations, abatement must occur within the mutually agreed upon time period.
Humanist	Protecting the safety and health of employees is the humanitarian thing to do—a company's moral obligation—regardless of legal obligation.
Public perception	Public perceptions about the company's attitude toward its employees can affect the market for its products.
Employee/labor relations	Employee involvement is a major tool in achieving quality safety and health. Consider areas in which employees can have a positive impact on safety performance.

A written corporate safety and health policy should address these issues:

- Management intent
- Scope of activities covered (on the job only, or off-time activities, too?)
- Assignment of responsibility and accountability
- A commitment to provide professional safety and health support

Safety and health professionals provide program direction, interpretation and technical assistance. They develop workplace safety and health procedures/standards, maintain program performance oversight and, in many instances, coordinate the safety and health effort. Safety and health professionals often assist in the selection, development and implementation of safety and health training programs for both management and non-management employees.

Managers and supervisors play a key role in safety and health performance. They make safety and health policy a reality by incorporating safety and health practices in both the physical workplace and in all tasks and processes on a planned, ongoing basis. They need to consider safety and health in the planning and decision-making process and not "after the fact."

First-line supervisors have direct responsibility for implementing the safety and health program. As members of "management," they enforce safety and health work practices and procedures and provide their subordinates with adequate and appropriate on-the-job training. They can most directly monitor conditions and performance and must be accountable for meeting performance goals.

Employees are being given more and more responsibility in program implementation. By participating through various company-sponsored means such as teams and committees, they help set performance goals, develop measures to gauge performance and have a vested interest in the program's success.

Performance Objectives

Performance objectives help employees and management meet their safety and health responsibilities by providing a target or benchmark against which to measure their progress. Procedures (an action plan) should be designed to help achieve objectives. The action plan consists of a series of steps that, when accomplished, will result in achieving the performance objective. The following are examples of performance objectives; the action plan necessary to achieve the objectives will vary depending on the nature of the business.

Senior managers

- Realize no increases in insurance rates due to preventable causes in the next fiscal year.
- Decrease overall safety and health-related fines by 50% in the next fiscal year.

Managers

- Achieve 100% reporting of incidents.

- Assure that labels in compliance with the OSHA Hazard Communication Standard are on all containers within one week.

Supervisors

- Decrease department rate of incidents by 60% for the next fiscal year.

Performance Standards and Guidelines

Safety and health policy is brought to life through measurable objectives that reflect management's expectations for safety performance. Objectives provide a benchmark to gauge safety and health performance and measure progress as well as identify areas for performance improvement.

Company standards must reflect relevant regulations, such as those from OSHA and MSHA. To be effective, internally established company standards should also reflect current industry best practices. Several standards-setting organizations in the United States and abroad establish voluntary standards for safety and health as well as for other areas of business (for example, quality). These organizations include the American Conference of Governmental Industrial Hygienists (ACGIH), the American National Standards Institute (ANSI), the American Society for Testing and Materials (ASTM), the National Fire Protection Association (NFPA), the European Committee for Standardization (CEN), and the International Organization for Standardization (ISO).

To be effective, company-established standards must be specific, address a defined objective and task and be measurable. Two examples of company-established performance standards are:

- The supervisor will inspect Area 1 weekly according to Standard Operating Procedure SH55.

- All new employees will be given a one-day health and safety orientation within 30 days of employment at this facility.

Conformance to standards

Performance standards can be met only when the affected individuals understand the expectations and how to achieve them, and are given the tools to do so. Procedures specify the way to accomplish the job safely and effectively. Procedures should be established for every work task.

Data collection and analysis are used to measure progress toward achieving safety and health goals. Performance measurement provides the most effective feedback and the key to continuous improvement. Numbers and measurements provide something tangible that management can respond to and use. Safety and health data and information collection are discussed in Element 6.

Traditional safety measurements, such as incidence rates, measure injuries and illnesses that have already occurred—i.e., failures of the safety and health program. Traditional safety measurements are results-oriented and measure:

- incidence rates

  □ total recordable injuries/illnesses per 200,000 hours worked

  □ days away from work per 200,000 hours worked

- workers' compensation costs (usually calculated as an average per employee)

Task performance specifications or standards focus on the process of successfully and safely performing an operation. Say, for example, that the organization has a standard requiring that all employees undergo a safety and health orientation within the first 30 days of employment. A procedure would need to be developed to address the content of the orientation, its length and depth, any hands-on exercises, documentation (to verify that the employee had satisfactorily completed the orientation) and criteria for further follow-up or refresher training. The specified documentation would need to be sufficient to monitor compliance with the standard and to help monitor achievement of the goal that spawned the standard. The goal behind the standard and the procedure must always be kept firmly in mind. Standards should also specify action levels and associated actions for noncompliance.

Compliance with the standard could be measured by examining employee records and documentation from the orientation. Deviations from the standard (employees not undergoing orientation or completing the orientation past the 30-day standard) should be investigated and the causes identified. Occasional deviations might have understandable causes. But repeated deviations may indicate a systematic problem and the need for corrective measures.

Accountability

Employees at all levels must accept responsibility for doing their jobs safely and be accountable for meeting safety performance goals. Canadian and European safety and health standards hold employees directly accountable for unsafe practices. In the United States, employers and employees are accountable under OSHA for maintaining safe work conditions and practices. Moreover, employees are directly accountable to OSHA for unsafe work practices despite adequate and appropriate training.

Although the reward for working safely is in not becoming injured or ill, success in meeting performance goals should carry with it the possibility of recognition. Recognition can be as simple as a compliment or an employee's name posted on the lunchroom bulletin board. It can also take the form of bonuses, paid days off or salary increases.

Managers can be accountable directly through their budgets for workers' compensation and insurance costs attributable to operations under their control. Organizations may assign a fixed dollar amount to an incident, based on an industry average. This dollar amount is charged back to the department.

Failure to meet safety and health performance standards sends a clear message that a problem exists that must be corrected. Companies should investigate the cause of not meeting a performance standard and implement corrective actions—e.g., more effective training, modification of the standard to be more realistic, more effective hazard control measures, more effective communication of goals and expectations and, when warranted, disciplinary action procedures.

Performance Reviews and Appraisals

Performance reviews are a formal, comprehensive way to evaluate the success of the safety and health (or any) program. Performance reviews are more objective when hard performance data is used to evaluate total compliance with safety standards and to identify systemic problems with the program. The evaluations are based on input from inspections, audits, data summaries, and other reports.

Communicating the results

Safety and health professionals should communicate the findings of performance reviews in writing to senior management, which must be aware of the successes, problems, and needs of the safety and health program. Performance reports should do more than just report injury, illness, and incident frequencies and other statistics; they should be interpreted to clearly define problems and provide recommendations for improvement. The frequency of performance reviews should be specified and the information made available.

Inadequate communication is frequently at the root of poor performance. Therefore, performance results in some form should be communicated company-wide. If there are problems meeting performance standards, the employees in those areas may have insight into why and suggestions on how to improve performance. Communicating the performance results gives all involved employees needed feed-back. Even if the results are not great, they will show whatever progress has been made and point a direction for continuous improvement.

There are numerous vehicles for communicating performance results to employees, including performance bulletin boards (updated weekly to show performance and compared to the same period the year before), monthly newsletters with more detailed comparisons of safety performance; reports and regularly scheduled safety meetings.

Safety Performance Management Review

Safety performance management begins with a sound safety and health policy that mandates adherence to standards and assigns accountability. Safety performance is driven by a set of established procedures designed to accomplish work tasks efficiently and safely. Workers, supervisors and managers must all understand and comply with the procedures. The worksheet that follows can be used to assess your organization's safety performance program and establish a baseline for improvement.

Table 3 - 2. Safety Performance Management Review

| Issues/Questions | In Place | | | Action Plan |
	Yes	No	Partially	(if answer is "No" or "Partially")
3.1 Does the organization have a safety and health policy that addresses: ■ management intent? ■ scope of activities covered? ■ lines of responsibility? ■ assignment of accountability? ■ a commitment to use safety and health professionals for technical support? ■ safety committees and their function? ■ a delegation of authority mechanism for establishing standards?				
3.2 Is adequate funding available for necessary analyses and reporting?				
3.3 Does management review performance reports and provide feedback?				
3.4 Is there an organizational chart with responsibility/authority lines for safety performance management?				

TABLE 3 - 2. SAFETY PERFORMANCE MANAGEMENT REVIEW Continued

| Issues/Questions | In Place | | | Action Plan |
	Yes	No	Partially	(if answer is "No" or "Partially")
3.5 Is a mechanism in place for performance accountability?				
3.6 Is employee input solicited for developing performance standards and measures?				
3.7 Have performance standards been developed for all tasks?				
3.8 Have procedures been designed to safely carry out each task?				
3.9 Have measures been developed to monitor compliance with performance standards?				
3.10 Is compliance with performance standards monitored and reviewed on a regular basis? Is the frequency adequate?				

TABLE 3 - 2. SAFETY PERFORMANCE MANAGEMENT REVIEW Continued

Issues/Questions	In Place Yes	No	Partially	Action Plan (if answer is "No" or "Partially")
3.11 Are results of performance management compliance communicated to management (including senior management)?				
3.12 Are results of performance communicated to involved employees?				

References

Book

National Safety Council. *Accident Prevention Manual for Business & Industry: Administration & Programs,* 10th ed. Itasca, IL: NSC, 1992.

Articles

Ballard J. Safety in the new Europe. *Occupational Hazards,* March 1992.

Crall MJ. LaShier SA. Management accountability: allocating costs of unsafe work motivates managers. *Business Insurance,* Sept. 28, 1992.

Ezell CW. Safety management: a new and better way? *Occupational Hazards,* October 1992.

Jones SE. The key issues of safety and health. *Occupational Hazards,* May 1991.

Krause TR, et al. Measuring safety performance: the process approach. *Occupational Hazards,* June 1991.

Minter SG. Creating the safety culture. *Occupational Hazards,* August 1991.

Shapiro S. Global health, safety standards. *Business Insurance,* May 10, 1993.

Sheehan DB. Safety performance goals—the planning process. *Occupational Hazards,* November 1992.

Government Publications

State of California. *Developing a Workplace Safety and Health Program,* Document CS-1. Sacramento, CA: State of California, 1986.

U.S. General Accounting Office. *Occupational Safety and Health: Differences Between Program in the United States and Canada,* GAO/HRD-94-15FS. Washington, DC: U.S. GAO, December 1993.

Packaged Training Program

National Safety Council. Agenda 2000® Safety Health Environment Program. Itasca, IL: NSC, 1992.

Report

Breitenberg M. *Questions and Answers on Quality, the ISO 9000 Standard Series, Quality System Registration, and Related Issues,* NISTIR 4721. Washington, DC: U.S. Department of Commerce, Technology Administration, National Institute of Standards and Technology, 1993.

EXECUTIVE SUMMARY — ELEMENT 4

Regulatory compliance is the driving force behind most safety and health programs. Regulatory authorities in the United States and around the world often have differing safety and health requirements.

The regulatory framework for safety and health includes requirements from numerous authorities, including the U.S. government and individual states. Many countries impose safety and health regulations on companies doing business within their borders. The major agencies involved in developing and enforcing U.S. safety and health regulations include the Occupational Safety and Health Administration and the Mine Safety and Health Administration.

Effective regulatory compliance requires staying informed about current regulatory requirements and anticipating future issues. Among the information sources for regulatory information are the *Federal Register,* periodicals, and computer services.

Compliance should be considered only a minimum standard. Successful safety and health programs go beyond compliance and strive to manage risk to worker safety and health.

4

REGULATORY COMPLIANCE MANAGEMENT

Successful safety and health programs feature an effective mechanism to help manage compliance issues. Regulations are legal requirements established by government to control actions, conduct or procedures. Safety and health regulations address the physical aspects of the workplace in addition to the administration and management of a safe work environment.

Regulatory authorities include federal (or national), provincial or state, or local governments; individual countries or unified groups of governments (the European Union [EU], for example). Regulations have behind them the force of law. Regulatory authorities inspect businesses to ensure compliance through voluntary or forced means.

Failure to comply with international standards may prevent a company from doing business in other countries. Company offices/facilities in Europe, as well as exports to Europe, are required to comply with EU standards. Although many European standards are advisory in nature and not easily enforceable, they are often stricter than those in the United States.

Compliance should be viewed as a minimum, "broad brush" concept. Often regulations are not specific or comprehensive enough to address the multitude of actual hazards. Therefore, the compliance program should be only one aspect of an organization's safety and health program. Whether noncompliance is recognized through an internal audit or during a compliance inspection, it should be investigated and corrected.

A successful safety and health program addresses both job-related hazards and compliance activities. Success must be expressed in terms of both improved employee safety and health and compliance with legal/regulatory objectives.

A comprehensive prevention system addresses these issues:

- Design, construction and maintenance of the physical workplace
- Management of safety and health issues
- Performance and actions of employees
- Regulatory compliance

A formal mechanism to manage regulatory compliance issues should be in place to make sure existing and new regulations are adequately addressed.

Regulatory compliance management involves:

- keeping informed about the changing U.S. and international laws and regulations
- analyzing and applying appropriate regulations to the workplace
- monitoring compliance through self-assessment techniques

Identifying Applicable Standards

In the United States, safety and health are regulated by federal, state and local governing bodies. The primary federal safety and health law for business and industry is the Occupational Safety and Health Act of 1970 (OSHAct). The law (84 Statute 1593) was enacted to "assure ... every working man and woman in the Nation safe and healthful working conditions and to preserve our human resources" (OSHAct Preamble).

Standards under the OSHAct are established by the Occupational Safety and Health Administration (OSHA). OSHA standards address specification (machine guarding, egress, hazard communication, etc.) and performance (first-aid supplies, training, medical surveillance, etc.) issues.

The OSHA standards incorporate, by reference, previously established voluntary standards developed by industry and government research and standard-setting organizations, including the following organizations:

- American Conference of Government Industrial Hygienists (ACGIH)
- American National Standards Institute (ANSI)
- American Petroleum Institute (API)
- American Society for Testing and Materials (ASTM)
- National Fire Protection Association (NFPA)
- National Institute for Occupational Safety and Health (NIOSH)
- Underwriters Laboratories (UL)
- U.S. Department of Commerce
- U.S. Public Health Service

OSHA and the Environmental Protection Agency (EPA)

The OSHAct addresses the safety and health of a company's employees. Several environmental laws—particularly the Resource Conservation and Recovery Act (RCRA), the Comprehensive Environmental Response, Compensation and Liability Act (CERCLA, commonly known as Superfund) and the Clean Air Act—address the safety and health of the surrounding community. Occupational and environmental safety and health are often closely interrelated, and coordination between the two sets of laws is crucial to ensure effective compliance (see also Element 12—Environmental Management). The EPA and OSHA have a memorandum of understanding that addresses the interrelationship of occupational and environmental health and safety compliance schemes. This cooperation is designed to ensure standardization of compliance issues and prevention of redundancy and conflicting requirements.

The Mine Safety and Health Act

The Mine Safety and Health Act of 1977 (MSHA) requires mine operators to comply with safety and health standards implemented under the Act and sets forth numerous rights for mine workers, including specialized training. Standards under MSHA are included in 30 CFR 1-199. Proposed and new standards and regulations are published in the *Federal Register*. Like those under the OSHAct, regulations under the Mine act are subject to public comment before they are finalized.

State and Local Programs

Section 18(H) of the OSHAct allows states to establish their own plans for implementation and enforcement. Some states establish and enforce their own standards; some enforce federal standards. In states without state plans, the federal government enforces federal standards. State plans are required to be "at least as effective" as the federal program. State laws must include all issues and standards addressed by the federal program. Those standards not addressed in a state plan must then be enforced under the federal OSHA. OSHA must approve all state plans, which must undergo a three-year trial period to make sure they are effective.

Local governments may also impose fire and electrical codes, building codes, etc., that may have an impact on safety and health.

International Regulations and Standards

The European Union

The European Union (EU) comprises numerous European countries and was established to remove trade barriers within Europe and achieve a "single internal market." In 1989, the EU adopted a framework for workplace safety and health standards. Called the Framework Directive, it establishes some general principles for workplace safety and health. "Daughter directives" have since been adopted by the EU to set forth more specific regulatory requirements under the Framework Directive, including indoor air quality, video displays, personal protective equipment, etc. The intention of EU safety and health regulations is to standardize safety and health requirements across Europe, so that one unified standard may take the place of individual national standards. When possible, existing international standards are used to formulate directives. Member countries enact legislation to implement and enforce each directive.

Canada

While workplace safety and health regulations in the United States are federally controlled, there is no comprehensive national safety and health law in Canada. Safety and health laws and regulations are established and enforced by individual provinces. Funding for safety and health programs comes directly from employers. There is a substantial focus on employee participation and responsibility, and employees can be given the same penalties as employers for violating safety and health regulations.

Canadian inspectors have unlimited access to the workplace, and they have the authority to immediately shut down a work process that poses an imminent threat to the safety and health of employees.

Mexico

In Mexico, the regulatory authority rests with the General Directorate of Medicine and Safety in the Workplace (DGMST) under the Mexican Secretary for Labor and Social Welfare. The federal government has enforcement responsibility for safety and health, with some assistance from state authorities. Like those in Canada, Mexican employees are liable for safety and health violations and can be fined.

Staying Informed

Regulations are constantly being revised. New OSHA and other federal agency regulations are proposed frequently, while new directives and standards are being adopted by the EU. Achieving and maintaining compliance depends on continuously tracking regulations, analyzing their impact and responding. New, modified and proposed U.S. regulations are published in the *Federal Register*. For organizations in highly regulated industries, careful tracking of the *Federal Register* is an important routine and the best way to stay abreast of U.S. federal regulations. Many large companies employ full-time regulatory professionals to keep them informed of applicable new and proposed regulations. The regulations are sometimes difficult to understand and interpret, even for technically trained professionals. And for a company dependent on staying in compliance, assigning a knowledgeable safety and health professional to track the *Federal Register* is a must.

The *Federal Register and Code of Federal Regulations* are readily available via computer modem and on CD-ROM and disk for the computer. Computer versions of the regulations can be searched by word or topic, which simplifies the job of identifying pertinent regulations. Although these electronic documents are more expensive than the paper versions, organizations that must comply with numerous regulations may save considerable time and (in the long run) money by using these innovative tools. Up-to-date information on international standards is also available through on-line computer networks. Subscribing to and reading safety and health professional journals will also help organizations stay informed about new regulatory developments in the United States, Canada, Mexico, Europe and elsewhere. The *Barbour Index* contains a reference source and accompanying microfile on legislation, standards, codes of practice and reports applicable to the United Kingdom. Journals are also a good source of information about what is considered "best practice," even though standards addressing the same subject may not be available. In addition, the U.S. Export Service can provide specific information on directives, standards and regulations that affect particular exports.

Even if the organization does not have the luxury of a full-time regulatory staff, compliance help is plentiful and not necessarily costly. Individual states often provide free consulting services. Trade and professional associations specific to the company's industry usually keep track of relevant regulations and proposals. They offer technical information, low- or no-cost consulting services and advice. Service organizations such as the National Safety Council can also provide the support needed to keep up to date on regulations and standards. Several publishing firms, including the Bureau of National Affairs and Commerce Clearing House, for example, publish condensed versions of U.S. and international regulations and standards, including interpretations. From a management perspective, the important activity is to develop a protocol for staying informed on applicable regulations. Companies should delegate specific responsibility for tracking regulations and establish a mechanism for communicating information to potentially affected departments about new, modified or proposed regulations. This task is commonly assigned to the organization's safety and health department.

Assessing Compliance

A self-assessment, or a voluntary assessment conducted by a third party, is the best tool for assessing the level of compliance. In some cases, an organization may utilize in-house expertise in assessing compliance. Computer software programs are available to assess compliance and recommend actions that address deficiencies. State agencies and OSHA also have published compliance checklists in various forms.

Numerous private consulting firms also are available to provide comprehensive compliance assistance. Typically, these firms spend one or more days thoroughly reviewing operations, facilities and records to assess compliance with applicable standards. The consultant identifies all potential violations and recommends remedial actions. Often the consulting firm can help the company implement and evaluate the effectiveness of the corrective action. (A more detailed discussion of assessments, audits and evaluations is included in Element 14.)

Through state agencies, OSHA provides on-site consulting services to help companies identify and address hazardous conditions. The service includes a walk-through inspection. Identified violations are not subject to fines on the basis of this voluntary walk-through. During the inspection, the consultant identifies applicable standards and how they apply to the company's operations, points out apparent violations and makes recommendations to correct problems. The visit is followed up with a written report. Subsequent to the consulting visit, the company must correct the suspected violations or be cited.

Priority is given to small companies (fewer than 150 employees), those less able to afford private consulting firms. The service is free of charge. OSHA consultants will assess only compliance with OSHA and not adherence to European or other international standards.

The compliance assessment should focus on administrative (paper) issues as well as the physical aspects of the facility. Many violations found by compliance inspectors are related to administrative failures involving record-keeping completeness and accuracy. Companies need to evaluate training records, Material Safety Data Sheets, written programs (e.g., as required by the OSHA Hazard Communication Standard) and medical records, as well as compliance with hazard standards.

The assessment should identify causes for the noncompliance. It will be difficult to effectively correct a compliance problem without understanding the cause. After the assessment is completed, problems should be addressed in order of priority. It will take time to correct all the inadequacies; therefore, those that are potentially the most serious (would cause the greatest loss) should be addressed first.

Compliance Management Review

Continuous improvement is the guiding philosophy behind many quality standards and the "world's best practice" approach of the European Union. Senior management must make a commitment to, at a minimum, comply with all applicable standards and regulations, and establish a structure for accomplishing the task. Then the company should target improvement beyond minimal compliance. Use the following worksheet to review your organization's regulatory compliance management.

TABLE 4 - 1. COMPLIANCE MANAGEMENT REVIEW

| Issues/Questions | In Place | | | Action Plan |
	Yes	No	Partially	(if answer is "No" or "Partially")
4.1 Company safety and health policy mandates (at least) compliance with all federal, state and local standards.				
4.2 Management understands the financial implications of noncompliance.				
4.3 Adequate funding is allocated to assess compliance and, if necessary, hire consultants to assist.				
4.4 Management provides funds to subscribe to regulatory services, join associations, and attend seminars to keep up to date on new regulations and standards.				
4.5 Compliance management has been delegated to a responsible department or individual.				

TABLE 4 - 1. COMPLIANCE MANAGEMENT REVIEW Continued

Issues/Questions	In Place Yes	No	Partially	Action Plan (if answer is "No" or "Partially")
4.6 The organization currently follows procedures to track applicable regulations.				
4.7 The organization periodically and regularly conducts self-assessments.				
4.8 If the organization conducts business outside the United States, it has contacted the relevant countries for regulatory information and guidance.				

References

Books

Industrial Accident Prevention Association. *Developing Your Health and Safety Policy and Program: A Guide for Employers.* Toronto: IAPA, 1992. (This organization also publishes numerous publications on compliance with Canadian safety and health regulations.)

National Safety Council. *Accident Prevention Manual for Business & Industry: Administration and Programs,* 10th ed. Itasca, IL: NSC, 1992.

Government Publications

State of California. *Developing a Workplace Safety and Health Program,* Document CS-1. Sacramento, CA: State of California,1986.

Superintendent of Documents. Annual list of *Toxic Substances, Directory of Federal Agencies, Federal Register, OSHA Field Operations Manual, Occupational Safety and Health Act of 1970 (PL 91-596), Occupational Safety and Health Regulations, Title 29 Code of Federal Regulations.* Washington, DC: U.S. GPO.

U.S. General Accounting Office. *Occupational Safety and Health: Differences Between Program in the United States and Canada,* GAO/HRD-94-15FS. Washington, DC: U.S. GAO, December 1993.

U.S. Department of Labor, Occupational Safety and Health Administration. *OSHA: Your Workplace Rights in Action,* OSHA 3023. Washington, DC: U.S. GPO, 1986.

Articles

Ballard J. Safety in the new Europe. *Occupational Hazards,* March 1992.

Everly M. Are you ready for 1993? *Health & Safety at Work* (England), January 1993.

Ezell CW. Safety management: a new and better way? *Occupational Hazards,* October 1992.

Jones SE. The key issues of safety and health. *Occupational Hazards,* May 1991.

Mahler K. Europe, the OH&S leader. *Occupational Health and Safety* (England), October 1990.

Vogel C. EC '92: here comes a new set of rules. *Safety & Health,* March 1992.

Periodicals

Bureau of National Affairs. *Occupational Safety and Health Reporter* (weekly compilation of proposed and final regulations and summaries of relevant court cases).

Packaged Training Program

National Safety Council. Agenda 2000® Safety Health Environment Program. Itasca, IL: NSC, 1992.

*E*XECUTIVE SUMMARY — *ELEMENT 5*

The goal of occupational health services is to protect the health and well-being of employees. Different companies have different needs, and occupational health programs will vary in complexity from simple first-aid services to a comprehensive set of off- and on-the-job medical and health education services. The following features are characteristic of occupational health programs.

- A successful occupational health program requires the involvement of medical and technical professionals with specialized training in work-related injuries and illnesses.

- All occupational health programs must provide for basic response to occupational illnesses and injuries. Most organizations address this need through a combination of on-site and easily accessible external services. First-aid services should be available when timely medical treatment is not otherwise available and to provide prompt treatment for minor injuries.

- Periodic medical examinations are sometimes required to make sure the employee and the job are medically compatible. Where incompatibilities exist, work restrictions will exist and modifications in work procedures, equipment or process may be necessary to accommodate the employee. Medical evaluations are frequently given before new or transferred employees are placed in a given job. Accurate and complete medical records are crucial for monitoring the health and well-being of employees.

Element 5

OCCUPATIONAL HEALTH

The occupational health program is an integral part of an organization's total safety and health effort. The goal of occupational health is to identify, evaluate and control exposure to health hazards of the job and to assure proper treatment of work-related ailments and injuries. At a minimum, the program should address the immediate needs of injured or ill employees on the job through adequate first aid and response to emergencies. In the absence of a doctor's office, clinic or hospital near the workplace, employers must provide adequately trained and equipped personnel to render first aid to injured employees.

Management must determine the scope and nature of the company's occupational health program and allocate the resources to provide the appropriate services. The scope and nature of the program will depend on the size and nature of the organization's business, the types of activities performed and the available budget.

Management, safety and health professionals should develop program goals and establish functions, programs, procedures and activities to meet the company's occupational health goals. Management's continuing support will fuel the program's credibility and establish its authority.

The program should be monitored as it is implemented to identify areas for improvement. Particularly as a company grows and the face of its work force changes, its needs for occupational health services also will change.

Although the primary focus of most occupational health programs is on the health and well-being of employees on the job, occupational health is also affected by the employees' lives away from work. Injuries and illness resulting from off-the-job activities and lifestyles may diminish a person's health to the point where occupational demands can more easily cause or exacerbate an existing health condition. A fully successful occupational health program promotes the health and well-being of employees both on and off the job. Off-hours health issues can be addressed through physical conditioning and wellness programs, screening for common health problems, such as increased cholesterol and high blood pressure, and educational materials on such topics as healthy lifestyles.

Every company has different occupational health needs, depending on the nature of operations and the hazards they present. The company occupational health program should address maintenance of employee medical and exposure records, employee health services, employees' disabilities and rehabilitation, worksite exposure monitoring, periodic medical examinations and medical surveillance as appropriate to the activities and operations taking place at the facility.

Occupational Health Professionals

Occupational health services are provided by specialized health professionals, including occupational health physicians, occupational health nurses, industrial hygienists and health physicists.

Occupational physicians

Occupational physicians are MDs with specialized training in work-related diseases, illnesses and injuries. Depending on the hazards and nature of operations and the size and complexity of the occupational health program, a company may need the services of a full-time, part-time or consulting physician. Many companies contract physicians' services through local occupational medicine clinics. Clinics may also provide placement and other more specialized physical examinations, treatment of injuries and other consulting services.

Occupational health nurses

Occupational health nurses have specialized training in work-related illnesses and injuries. Occupational health nurses work alongside occupational health physicians to develop and maintain a company's occupational health program. In addition to treating routine occupational illnesses and injuries under the direction of the occupational health physician, occupational health nurses often are responsible for filing workers' compensation claims, maintaining employee medical records and educating employees on work and non-work-related health issues. Although occupational health nurses can provide many health services, they cannot take the place of a physician in diagnosing and treating serious work-related illnesses and injuries.

Industrial hygienists

Industrial hygienists are trained to anticipate, identify and evaluate physical, chemical and biological health hazards in the workplace and recommend control procedures for these hazards. They maintain their skills through continuing study and professional certification. Some hygienists have training in specialized disciplines such as epidemiology, toxicology, acoustics or ventilation systems. Industrial hygienists use sensitive instruments to measure exposure levels. Depending on an organization's needs, it may use either in-house industrial hygienists or contract with outside hygienists available through insurance companies or private consulting firms. After identifying a hazard, the industrial hygienist evaluates the degree of exposure and severity of impact on employees. After evaluating the hazard, the industrial hygienist recommends a means for controlling exposure or eliminating the hazard.

Health physicists

Health physics is a discipline dedicated to protecting humans and the environment from radiation hazards. Health physicists are employed by organizations to identify, evaluate and address radiation hazards in the workplace. Radioactive materials are used in many occupational settings. Some of these include:

- hospitals and medicine (radioactive materials are used in diagnostics, nuclear medicine, radiology, cancer treatment)

- utilities (nuclear power plants)

- industrial radiography operations (to diagnose structural defects)

- manufacturing facilities that utilize x rays as part of quality control operations

- biomedical research facilities (radioactive materials are used to mark and trace biological materials as they are metabolized)

Organizations that use radioactive materials should have an effective radiation safety program. A radiation safety officer should be appointed to oversee the program, provide education to employees exposed to radioactive materials and assure compliance with monitoring, record keeping and exposure control programs.

Employee Health Services

Health services provided on site should be placed in a dedicated location within the facility. The health service location should be private and clean, with adequate space to treat multiple cases at the same time and allow privacy for male and female patients. The health service space should have hot and cold running water and toilet facilities and should be adequately ventilated. Ideally, the clinical area should consist of a waiting room, a treatment room, and a consultation room. Larger facilities may also have rehabilitation areas, dressing areas or conference rooms, and facilities for taking x rays and performing laboratory tests and rehabilitation.

First Aid

First aid is the immediate care given to an injured or suddenly ill person. It consists of providing temporary care until proper medical treatment, if needed, is given.

All injured or suddenly ill employees should receive first-aid treatment, no matter how minor or serious the injury or illness. All injuries and illnesses must be reported. Prompt reporting and treatment of injuries and sudden illnesses is important to make sure that proper attention is given to the victim and to ensure accurate workers' compensation reporting, MSHA reporting, and OSHA record keeping. Companies can also use the recorded information to help correct the cause of the injury in order to prevent recurrences. Since first-aid requirements vary outside the United States, companies should check with the country's Labor Ministry or Department for current requirements.

First-aid supplies approved by a physician as appropriate for the exposure and a trained first-aid provider are required when timely medical treatment is not otherwise available. The first-aid kit and supplies should be inspected regularly on a scheduled basis to make sure the supplies are replenished as needed and to replace all expired, out-of-date or nonworking supplies. Access to first-aid supplies should be restricted to the first-aid practitioner. No ingestible medications should be given to employees except under the supervision of a nurse or physician.

First-aid providers should provide only the services approved by the physician. In addition, all designated first-aid providers should be trained and maintain first-aid certification under a program approved by the appropriate government agencies and provided by an established organization such as the National Safety Council.

Medical Records

United States regulations require employers to maintain records that include employee exposures to toxic materials, radiation and high noise levels. The nature and extent of medical record-keeping requirements outside the United States vary. Companies should contact the country's Labor Ministry or Department for current requirements.

Medical records can be analyzed to set health standards, place employees in jobs consistent with any physical or other limitations, provide support documentation for insurance claims and make accurate diagnoses of illnesses. They also can be used to help monitor the effectiveness of the company's safety and health program and justify improvements in existing programs. Although medical records are useful in many ways to help evaluate and improve practices, procedures and conditions in the workplace, access to records must be strictly limited to health personnel and individual, personal confidentiality maintained.

Medical records can include the employee's medical history, the results of physical examinations and tests (including audiograms), descriptions of injuries and illnesses (and their diagnoses and treatment) and records of exposure to harmful or toxic agents. Exposure records report the history of the employee's exposure to the agent, describe the work conditions that may have resulted in the exposure and any other related information and contain relevant data from the MSDS. Depending on the nature of the exposure and the industry, medical and exposure records may need to be kept for up to 30 years past termination of a person's employment.

The medical record program should be established formally in writing. Companies must formally delegate and monitor authority and responsibility for keeping those records. The occupational health nurse or other health provider should maintain medical records, which should be considered an important professional responsibility. Sometimes, particularly when there are no full-time dedicated health professionals, medical records are kept by the personnel officer or equivalent. Medical records on individual employees must be kept in a location that is separate from other personnel records.

Procedures for recording, reporting, maintaining and retrieving records should be implemented and their effectiveness monitored. Storage locations for records, access procedures and confidentiality must all be addressed.

Employees with Disabilities

Employees with disabilities can often handle many job functions, depending upon their limitations. The occupational health team should work with these employees and other organized resources to find the safest and most effective approaches to performing the work tasks. (Additional discussion is provided in Element 13— Work Force Planning and Staffing.) Although the human resources department usually has the primary responsibility for placing and working with employees with disabilities, the occupational health physician and/or nurse should evaluate the employee to define limitations and work restrictions and then, in collaboration with other safety and health and related professionals, recommend ways to address or overcome the identified barriers where accommodations can be made.

Worksite Monitoring

Monitoring the workplace for health hazards is an integral part of a company's occupational health program. Monitoring identifies harmful and potentially harmful chemical, biological and physical agents and is used to evaluate the impact of these agents on employees' health. Several types of worksite monitoring can be conducted as part of the occupational health program. These include personal exposure monitoring, work area monitoring, biological monitoring and medical monitoring. These monitoring types are introduced in Element 1—Hazard Recognition, Evaluation and Control. In general, personal exposure and work area monitoring are conducted by industrial hygienists to evaluate the levels of potentially harmful agents in the workplace and determine the need for controls.

Biological monitoring requires evaluating bodily fluids (blood, urine, etc.) or tissues for the presence of harmful agents. Biological monitoring is usually performed by a physician equipped with a specialized laboratory to measure even extremely low levels of substances, including radioactive contaminants, in human tissue. Because some types of biological monitoring involve invasive procedures, it is used mainly when exposure potential and the hazard are severe enough to warrant such measures. Medical personnel conduct medical monitoring to evaluate the physical and psychological effects of potentially harmful agents. Medical monitoring may include taking medical and work histories, physical examinations, x rays and laboratory tests and testing hearing and vision. Monitoring records are helpful for identifying exposures to health hazards before they cause serious illness or injury to employees.

Periodic Medical Examinations and Medical Surveillance

Medical examinations are needed for a variety of reasons, including the following:

Preplacement. Preplacement examinations or preplacement evaluations are routinely made before hiring a new employee or transferring a current employee to another job. A medical exam establishes a new employee's medical condition and compares the physical condition of the employee with the documented requirements of the job. If preplacement physicals are performed on acceptable candidates for a particular position, they must be performed on *all* applicants and employees being considered for that position. The examination reveals whether the employee is medically qualified to perform the stated job tasks and whether the job is medically suitable for the employee. When the job and the condition of the employee are determined to be medically incompatible, the physician or other occupational health professional should recommend ways to modify the job tasks or equipment to accommodate the employee, which would be in accordance with the Americans With Disabilities Act (ADA). The physician should then perform periodic follow-up examinations to ensure that the job and the worker continue to be compatible. Information obtained in the examination must remain confidential.

Return to work after an illness or injury. A physical examination is often conducted when an employee returns to work after a prolonged illness. The objective is to determine whether the employee is able to perform all the required work activities immediately or whether work restrictions are applicable, which can allow for activities to be phased in gradually. The supervisor and the physician can work as a team with the employee to identify any modifications needed.

Exit examination. Exit examinations record the medical and health condition of the employee when he or she leaves employment. They provide feedback to the organization on the impact of job tasks on the medical condition of employees. By officially recording the medical condition of employees when they leave the company, exit examinations can provide medical documentation in case of any future legal claims.

Medical surveillance. Medical surveillance involves the ongoing monitoring of the entire work force to detect abnormalities. It is used particularly when employees may have been exposed to certain chemicals or other harmful agents such as lead, cadmium or noise in the workplace. At the preplacement physical examination, baseline levels of the relevant substances can be measured, often in blood or urine. These biological levels are periodically remeasured and compared to established standards to make sure the exposure stays below the standard. Increased levels or those that approach or exceed the standards may indicate a serious health hazard.

The frequency and scope of periodic medical examinations and the nature of medical surveillance will depend on the type of hazards to which employees are exposed and are often regulated by governmental agencies. In some cases, medical examinations might be provided for employees as a service—on a voluntary, annual basis, for example. In other cases, where exposure to specific hazardous agents is possible, regulations may require medical examinations at specified frequencies. The nature of the needed exam may vary, from drawing and analyzing blood for a targeted agent to taking x rays and conducting comprehensive examinations.

The occupational health program should define and specify in writing the conditions and criteria for periodic medical examinations and medical surveillance. Guidelines for conducting and maintaining medical surveillance records have been published by regulatory agencies and other organizations.

Worksite Health Promotion Programs

Worksite health promotion programs educate employees on living a healthy lifestyle both on and off the job. The emphasis in these "wellness" programs is on preventing disease. The payoff to the organization is a better informed and healthier work force, resulting in increased productivity, decreased absenteeism, lower turnover and potentially lower workers' compensation costs, plus possible decreases in medical insurance claims.

The health promotion program can focus on one issue, such as stress or hypertension, or may be a comprehensive program incorporating numerous aspects of physical and psychological well-being. The program may include informational materials, classes, workshops or counseling. Some companies provide exercise equipment or membership in a local health club as part of their health promotion program. Smaller organizations can create a health promotion program by coordinating or pooling resources with other companies (for example, several office-based organizations housed in the same building). Also, companies can often use community resources to provide health promotion programming. Fire departments and hospitals can often provide a combination of on-site and off-site services to educate and work with employees on wellness issues.

Occupational Health Review

Management directs and focuses the priorities of the occupational health program. The scope and nature of the program will depend on such considerations as legal requirements, how the organization views its responsibilities, its perception of sound business practices and its financial resources. Use the worksheet below to review your organization's occupational health program.

TABLE 5 - 1. OCCUPATIONAL HEALTH REVIEW

Issues/Questions	In Place			Action Plan
	Yes	No	Partially	(if answer is "No" or "Partially")
5.1 Has management established a formal occupational health program?				
5.2 Has management hired or contracted with a physician, nurse and/or hygienists as needed?				
5.3 Are hired or contracted occupational health personnel adequate in number, skills and training for workplace conditions?				

TABLE 5 - 1. OCCUPATIONAL HEALTH REVIEW Continued

| Issues/Questions | In Place | | | Action Plan |
	Yes	No	Partially	(if answer is "No" or "Partially")
5.4 Are accurate and complete medical records maintained? Are procedures in place for notification and reports involving injuries, illnesses, fatalities and exposures within the company as required by regulatory bodies?				
5.5 Does management address the special needs of employees with disabilities?				
5.6 Does management provide funding for continuing education and certification of occupational physicians, occupational health nurses and industrial hygienists who are on staff?				
5.7 Does management support and fund wellness, educational and off-the-job health programs?				

TABLE 5 - 1. OCCUPATIONAL HEALTH REVIEW Continued

Issues/Questions	In Place Yes	No	Partially	Action Plan (if answer is "No" or "Partially")
5.8 Does management support efforts to maintain the mental well-being of employees through an employee assistance program?				
5.9 Does management provide counseling on lifestyle problems, including drug and alcohol abuse?				
5.10 Are there established, effective procedures to ensure confidentiality of medical records?				
5.11 Are employees with disabilities identified?				

TABLE 5 - 1. OCCUPATIONAL HEALTH REVIEW Continued

| Issues/Questions | In Place | | | Action Plan |
	Yes	No	Partially	(if answer is "No" or "Partially")
5.12 Are occupational health professionals part of a team for evaluating and accommodating employees with disabilities?				
5.13 Is worksite monitoring conducted as required by governmental or professional standards?				
5.14 Are procedures to conduct monitoring in writing, and are they evaluated for effectiveness?				
5.15 Have medical examinations and medical surveillance needs been evaluated? Are procedures in place and effective?				

References

Books

A.M. Best Company. *Best's Safety Directory*, vol. II. Oldwick, NJ: A.M. Best Company, 1992.

Bird FE, Germain GL. *Practical Loss Control Leadership*, 2nd ed. Logansville, GA: International Loss Control Institute, 1990.

Cralley LJ, Cralley LV. *Patty's Industrial Hygiene*. New York: John Wiley & Sons, 1985.

National Safety Council. *Occupational Health and Safety*, 2nd ed. Itasca, IL: NSC, 1994.

National Safety Council. *Accident Prevention Manual for Business and Industry, Administration & Programs*, 10th ed. Itasca, IL: NSC, 1992.

Petersen D. *Safety Management: A Human Approach*, 2nd ed. Goshen, NY: Aloray Inc., 1988.

Articles

Hans M. Preemployment physicals and the ADA. *Safety & Health*, February 1992.

Hogan JC. Developing job-related preplacement medical examinations. *Journal of Occupational Medicine*, July 1987.

Howe HF. Organization and operation of an occupational health program. *Journal of Occupational Medicine*, June 1975, July 1975, August 1975.

Packaged Training Program

National Safety Council. Agenda 2000® Safety Health Environment Program. Itasca, IL: NSC, 1992.

Government Publication

U.S. General Accounting Office. *Occupational Safety and Health: Differences Between Program in the United States and Canada,* GAO/HRD-94-15FS. Washington, DC: U.S. GAO, December 1993.

U.S. Department of Commerce. *Comparison of Occupational Safety and Health Programs in the United States and Mexico: An Overview,* PB93-129963. Springfield, VA: U.S. Department of Commerce, 1992.

EXECUTIVE SUMMARY — ELEMENT 6

Information is the key to decision making in all areas of business. For safety and health purposes, data can be used to determine workplace hazards and to identify areas for improvement. Inspections, record keeping, injury/illness/incident investigations, industrial hygiene surveys and performance reviews all generate the information used to evaluate safety and health performance and improvement.

Injuries and illnesses cost organizations directly and indirectly. Quantifying injuries and illnesses in terms of dollars gives senior management a clear picture of their real cost.

Computers and analytical software often can be used to facilitate data collection and analyses. Computers can help manage large data bases and generate analyses and custom reports quickly and easily.

Element 6

INFORMATION COLLECTION

Information is the key to making sound decisions in all areas of business. Information on performance can be used to establish goals, plan for steady and continuous improvement and assess progress. Accurate and complete records are also critical in documenting adherence to standards and regulations.

In effective safety and health programs, performance goals are set and measured on an ongoing basis. Measurement helps define "how much" has been done and helps identify "how far" there is yet to go. Used as an evaluation tool, information should serve as a springboard for continuous improvement, helping to set sights on new goals and targets. The following components of successful safety and health programs can help generate information:

- inspections (self-inspections as well as compliance audits)
- regulatory and other record keeping
- injury/illness/incident investigations
- industrial hygiene surveys and other occupational health assessments
- performance reviews

Analysis of the information can identify problem areas and reveal trends that need management attention. Some data are useful in supporting requests to management for additional resources. Other data can be used as evidence that improvements are real and measurable.

Evaluating raw numbers and translating them into useful information have become much easier in the 1990s. Many companies use personal computers that can store extensive information in data bases. Readily available and inexpensive software can analyze the data and produce a wide variety of custom reports.

However, even the most sophisticated computer software is only as reliable as the input data and the knowledge and skill of the user. Reliable information and analyses are possible only through complete and accurate record keeping. Analyses based on incomplete or inaccurate records may yield incorrect and misleading conclusions. Therefore, the steps required to report and record information accurately and uniformly should be an important feature of written procedures for conducting investigations, inspections or other processes that provide data.

The following sections describe the information collection and analysis tools commonly used to evaluate and improve safety and health performance.

Cost Analysis

Cost versus benefit is the language of management. The most effective tool for showing management the cost-effectiveness of sound safety and health practices is safety performance defined in terms of cost to the company. An organization's accounting system must be designed to collect and isolate the needed cost data; otherwise, accurately translating safety and health performance into dollars will be largely a matter of guesswork. Translating injuries, illnesses and property damage into dollars and, likewise, translating prevention into terms of cost savings may be more meaningful to management than incidence rates. Demonstrating the positive financial effect of prevention makes a strong safety policy more than "just good policy"; it demonstrates good business sense.

One area of safety management most useful to measure is the cost of accidents—preventable occurrences that result in injury, property damage and other losses. (See Element 1 for a discussion of injury/illness/incident investigations.) Accident cost estimates include the cost of workers' compensation, payments for medical expenses and lost wages (indemnity). The total cost can be defined in terms of insured and uninsured costs. Workers' compensation costs along with fire and extended coverage losses are examples of insured costs. The following are examples of uninsured (and often less obvious) costs:

- Wages of employees who are nonproductive during their involvement with the incident

- Wages of injured parties in excess of workers' compensation payments

- Uninsured medical costs paid by the company

- Overtime needed to make up for lost production time or repairs

- Decreased output of recovering (but at work) injured employees

- Hiring and training costs

- Lower productivity for temporary or replacement employees

- Time chargeable to the incident spent on claims, record keeping, investigation and reporting

- Lost production

- Repair or scrap of damaged product

- Equipment and material repair and replacement costs

While they are less tangible and more difficult to estimate, management should also consider losses from any negative publicity, adverse customer relations, lowered employee morale, etc.

This type of cost analysis can be adapted and applied to any illness or injury situation.

Information Management

Maintaining a potentially huge amount of safety and health data could be a monumental task, depending upon the organization's size and its incident experience. Information collected during different activities may be related, and storing it in a format that allows easy integration and analysis would be useful.

When only a few records are involved, data can be efficiently and cost-effectively managed and analyzed manually. However, with large amounts of data, computer systems are invaluable for data management. Computers and applicable software can be an effective tool to manage injury/illness/incident information. Computers can offer these advantages:

- Storage and processing of large amounts of information

- Quick transmission of data across distances

- Production of a variety of custom reports in a variety of formats

- Rapid retrieval of information for reports and searches

- Improved accuracy and standardization

- More sophisticated analyses without great time expenditure

- Elimination of some paper files and manual record keeping

Computer technology changes so rapidly, and individual needs vary so widely, that it is impossible to provide current computer hardware and software specifications. In general, when thinking of purchasing a system, consider how the system will be used (perhaps in addition to safety and health applications), who will use the system and what hardware and software features are desirable. The chosen system should have sufficient storage space to maintain all data and speed adequate to retrieve and analyze it quickly.

Software to manage injury/illness/incident and other data is commercially available. Using these prepackaged computer programs simplifies information management. Although some companies choose to design their own incident management software systems, using prepackaged programs is convenient and costs less than hiring programmers to design a custom system. Generally, prepackaged software has been tested in the field and usually has readily accessible technical support.

The computer can be used to store and analyze many types of data, including:

- employee medical records

- training records

- inspection reports of workplace conditions

- illnesses and injuries (OSHA logs and other records)

- incidents that resulted in no losses

- workers' compensation claim data

Data base information can be used to generate many different types of analyses and reports showing both activity and performance. Reports, complete with computer-generated charts and graphics, can be communicated throughout the organization to inform everyone of safety and health progress.

Reports on Workplace Conditions

Information about workplace conditions is collected from various safety and health activities, including:

- self-inspections

- job safety analyses

- audits by others

- industrial hygiene surveys

- maintenance reports

The information taken as a whole, and analyzed along with injury/illness/incident information, can provide a detailed composite picture of workplace safety and health conditions. The information can be used independently to establish the baseline against which to measure performance. Used collectively, the data from these various sources can be used to help define high-hazard areas in the workplace that perhaps can be correlated with high incidence rates. This type of correlation can help prioritize plans for corrective action. For example, it can identify which areas in the facility have the following conditions:

- High injury/illness/incident occurrence/numerous or severe hazards (a serious problem and a high priority)

- High injury/illness/incident occurrence/no apparent hazards (This signifies a problem with the system used to identify workplace hazards, or that something unrelated to the physical workplace conditions is creating the high incidence.)

- Low injury/illness/incident occurrence/high hazard (injuries/illnessess/incidents "waiting to happen")

- Low injury/illness/incident occurrence/no uncontrolled hazards

This process of analysis and correlation is part of data analysis.

Data Analysis

Identifying injury and illness patterns can help define specific analysis needs. For example, is a high incidence of injuries associated with a particular piece of equipment or a certain procedure? Analysis of near-miss incidents in a specific department can identify a serious hazard waiting to cause a serious injury. Summaries can be compared between departments of a company or between companies within an industry. Comparing information with that of other companies engaged in a similar business can demonstrate how well your company is doing. For stronger validity, analysis requires large amounts of data.

Injury and illness incidence rates are commonly used to evaluate safety and health performance. Injury and illness incidence rates can be charted weekly, monthly or as needed by the nature of operations to examine trends over time. The most common incidence rate formulas used in the United States are those associated with OSHA record keeping:

- Total recordable injuries and illnesses

- Total cases involving days away from work

Incidence rates express the frequency of some occurrence compared to a standard reference. In OSHA's formula, frequency of occurrence is expressed as a ratio per 200,000 hours (100 person years) of exposure.

$$\text{Total recordable injury/ illness incidence rate} = \frac{\text{Total recordable injuries and illnesses} \times 200{,}000 \text{ hours (comparison base)}}{\text{Total hours worked (i.e., actual hours of exposure of a company or component being measured)}}$$

This rate quantifies the injury and illness experience of any defined group in an easy-to-understand, readily comparable form. The following additional evaluations can be made to identify the causes of injuries and illness.

- Injuries and illnesses by cause factors (lack of knowledge, training, procedures, etc.). This analysis requires accurate reporting. When many incidents fall into a few categories, the results may point to a few specific causes, which can then be corrected.

- Injuries and illnesses by level of employees' experience. This analysis identifies potential training or orientation problems. High incidence rates in experienced employees may signify complacency or sloppiness and indicate a need for emphasis on refresher training, or may indicate unresolved problems, such as with equipment or processes.

- Injuries and illness by time of day and shift. This analysis can indicate problems with fatigue, inadequate supervision on later shifts, etc.

- Injuries and illness by specific equipment and tools. This analysis may help identify specific processes, equipment and tools that may need updating or otherwise changing.

When examining month-to-month trends, it is important to identify factors that could account for incidence rate fluctuations. If an incident rate is unusually low (or high), qualify the data as to what could have caused the unusual month. Could inexperience of employees from a newly added work shift or fatigue from overtime work have contributed to the incidence rates for the corresponding periods?

Analysis information should be compiled into clear and meaningful reports to management that reflect performance and recommend actions for continued improvement.

Injury and Illness Case Analysis

OSHA does not require recording injuries that only need first aid. However, if first aid was administered but the injury involved loss of consciousness, restriction of motion or transfer to another job, then the injury is recordable. Companies interested only in compliance and not in getting the most from their safety and health programs will not investigate injuries or illnesses beyond those meeting the recordability requirement. However, companies with proactive, preventive programs make sure that all work-related injuries, exposures and illnesses that could be work-related are reported to management and investigated. It has long been known to management that when an accident occurs, the severity of a resulting injury or other loss will be largely a matter of chance. Therefore, loss prevention requires causal analysis of all accidents, regardless of severity, and incidents—those occurrences that, except for chance, could have resulted in injuries or other loss (commonly referred to as near misses).

OSHA Forms

OSHA recordable injuries and illnesses are recorded on OSHA forms or their equivalents. There are two forms:

- Form 200—Log and Summary of Occupational Injuries and Illnesses
- Form 101—Supplementary Record of Occupational Injuries and Illnesses

Any questions regarding OSHA injury and illness record keeping should be addressed to the OSHA area office serving the company's geographic location.

The OSHA Form 200 is used to:

- record basic information about the injury/illness and the person involved, and data concerning any resulting time lost from work, restricted duty or fatality
- annually provide a certified summary of a company's injury/illness experience

OSHA Form 101 is used to more fully describe injuries and illnesses recorded on OSHA Form 200. Both are available from all OSHA area offices.

The U.S. Bureau of Labor Statistics (BLS), with participation from some state labor departments, conducts an annual survey of occupational illnesses and injuries. Companies that are sampled must submit, along with other information, some of the injury and illness data contained in the OSHA 200 Log and the OSHA 101 Supplementary Record.

Canadian provinces also require collection of workplace illness and injury data. Some European countries require formal illness and injury data collection as well. The best source of information on data collection requirements is the provincial or national ministry of safety and health or ministry of labor.

Off-the-Job Injury Data

Injuries occurring away from work also affect a company's cost structure. For example, most employers incur group medical insurance costs, and some employers pay wages for time taken off during these medical absences. There can be additional uninsured costs incurred from off-the-job injuries just as there are for on-the-job injuries.

Collecting and analyzing off-the-job injury and illness data from insurance claim forms can help identify unsafe or unhealthy off-time activities that may affect the company. American National Standard ANSI Z16.3-1989 covers the recording and treatment of data for computing off-the-job incidence rates of full-time employees and presents a general basis for analyzing the reported injuries. Based on the results of the off-the-job injury and illness analyses, the employer may want to offer employees educational materials, counseling and other programs to promote a safe and healthy lifestyle.

Cost analyses of off-the-job injuries (see NSC Data Sheet I-601) can provide supporting evidence for off-the-job educational and safety and health programs. The effectiveness of off-the-job programs, considered by some to be "frills," can be measured in terms of cost savings to the company in other areas, such as employee turnover, absenteeism, insurance costs, etc.

Information Collection Review

Information collection is at the center of the continuous improvement process. Without collection of accurate and complete information, there can be no evaluation of experience or progress. Goals based on collection and evaluation of unreliable data may not be valid or attainable. Therefore, collecting, maintaining, and accurately analyzing reliable data is the foundation for improvement.

Establishing an effective information system requires a firm commitment of resources from senior management and its involvement in reading reports, providing input and feedback, and understanding the financial impact of safety and health improvement. Use the following worksheet to identify the information collection baseline and set goals for improved information collection.

TABLE 6 - 1. INFORMATION COLLECTION REVIEW

Issues/Questions	In Place Yes	No	Partially	Action Plan (if answer is "No" or "Partially")
6.1 Does management require data collection and analysis?				
6.2 Does management require, read and provide feedback on periodic occupational injury and illness reports and other related reports?				
6.3 Are sufficient resources allocated for data collection and analysis activities?				

TABLE 6 - 1. INFORMATION COLLECTION REVIEW Continued

Issues/Questions		In Place Yes	No	Partially	Action Plan (if answer is "No" or "Partially")
6.4	Does management compare company data to similar companies or between similar departments within the same company?				
6.5	Does management understand safety and health in terms of financial impact?				
6.6	Does management require off-the-job data and support an off-the-job-program?				
6.7	Does management post an annual OSHA Log summary by February 1 and leave it up for a minimum of one month?				
6.8	Does the safety and health department have access to a computer?				
6.9	Is computer hardware adequate to maintain records?				

TABLE 6 - 1. INFORMATION COLLECTION REVIEW Continued

Issues/Questions	In Place Yes	No	Partially	Action Plan (if answer is "No" or "Partially")
6.10 Has software been purchased for tracking and analysis of safety and health data?				
6.11 Are procedures in place for complete, timely, accurate and uniform data collection?				
6.12 Are data and records kept and updated on a routine and frequent basis?				
6.13 Is data on workplace conditions collected and used with other data to generate reports?				
6.14 Are inspection reports maintained for easy follow-up and analysis?				

References

Books

Bird FE, Germain GL. *Practical Loss Control Leadership.* Logansville, GA: International Loss Control Institute, 1990.

Grimaldi JV, Simonds RH. *Safety Management: Accident Cost and Control,* 5th ed. Homewood, IL: Richard D. Irwin, Inc., 1988.

National Safety Council. *Accident Prevention Manual for Business & Industry: Administration & Programs,* 10th ed. Itasca, IL: NSC, 1992.

National Safety Council. *Accident Facts.* Itasca, IL: NSC, 1993.

Peterson D. *Safety Management, A Human Approach.* Goshen, NY: Aloray, Inc., 1988.

Government Publications

U.S. Department of Labor, Bureau of Labor Statistics. *A Brief Guide to Recordkeeping Requirements for Occupational Injuries and Illnesses.* Washington, DC: 1986.

U.S. Department of Labor, Bureau of Labor Statistics. *Recordkeeping Guidelines for Occupational Injuries and Illnesses.* Washington, DC: 1986.

Article

Hughes MS. Europe's mixture of diverse customs poses challenge to EEC safety goals. *Occupational Health & Safety* (England), October, 1993.

Packaged Training Program

National Safety Council. Agenda 2000® Safety Health Environment Program. Itasca, IL: NSC, 1992.

Standard

American National Standards Institute. ANSI Z16.3-1989, "Injury Statistics—Employee Off-the-Job Injury Experience—Recording and Measuring."

Data Sheet

Data Sheet I-601. Off-the-Job Safety. Itasca, IL: NSC, 1986.

EXECUTIVE SUMMARY — ELEMENT 7

By involving employees in the decision-making process, management affords them a greater sense of "owning" the resulting policies. Ownership translates into increased acceptance of and support for those policies. Management can facilitate a cooperative effort to improve the safety and health program through employee participation.

The team structure that management chooses should fit its particular culture and organization. We discuss the basic concepts that support the successful formation of goal-oriented safety and health teams.

The safety and health committee is a form of employee involvement that is sometimes mandated by law and/or required by organized labor contracts. For this reason, we address committees separately in a discussion of issues common to committee organization, with special attention to union participation.

Management must also foster the involvement of individual workers who do not participate in team structures. Companies can use a number of tools to elicit individual input and cooperation.

Management should validate the value of employee involvement by routinely and formally recognizing those individuals or groups who have made significant contributions to safety and health.

Element **7**

■ ■ ■ ■ ■ ■ ■ ■ ■ ■ ■ ■ ■

EMPLOYEE INVOLVEMENT

In the dual surveys cited in the introduction to this manual, the National Safety Council asked safety and health professionals—in 1967 and again in 1992—for their opinions of the importance of various safety practices. Comparison of the two surveys shows that employee-management safety and health committees have emerged as a key element of the overall safety and health program. This increase reflects a shift in business philosophies toward greater emphasis on integrated management processes centered around team-building and employee empowerment.

Indeed, employee involvement in corporate safety and health programs is now perceived to be so important that safety and health committees are mandated by law in some states in the United States, and impending OSHA reform may well result in federally mandated committees. All provinces of Canada mandate joint employer-worker responsibility and accountability for occupational safety. In some provinces, the committee that determines provincial occupational safety standards is comprised equally of employer and worker representatives. In Europe, the language of the European Framework Directive speaks of "balanced participation and consultation" between employers and employees.

Clearly, governments and regulatory agencies are realizing that employees can and should be involved in business decisions affecting safety and health in the workplace—decisions that were once the sole province of management and support specialists such as safety/occupational health professionals and engineers.

Employee involvement in the safety and health program can be mandated; a cooperative spirit cannot. Management must first recognize the value of employee participation before it can successfully implement systems to foster it. The positive impact of employee involvement is obvious when we consider that the central objective of any safety and health program—preventing loss-producing incidents and illness—is attained largely through a high level of awareness of unsafe practices and occupational hazards and by sustained acceptance of policies and procedures designed to protect worker safety and health. Both awareness and acceptance must exist at all levels of the organization. Management nurtures such awareness and acceptance when it solicits, encourages and responds to input from all levels.

Employee involvement in all phases of the safety and health program—design, planning, implementation and evaluation—benefits both employees and management and enhances the continuous improvement process. Performance results improve through the cooperative exchange of knowledge and experience. Employees know from direct day-to-day experience where many unsafe practices and occupational hazards exist and, often, how to best address them. This empirical knowledge is invaluable to the corporate safety and health effort. Moreover, employees are far more likely to accept and commit to decisions and changes that are based on their own input and open communication with management.

No one structure is an ideal system for employee involvement in safety and health. Any good system must fit comfortably into the organization it serves. We will look at "teams," "circles" and other structures as viable options to safety and health committees. However, our real intent in this chapter is to examine the concepts that will support any employee involvement program—regardless of its formal setting—that is oriented toward results and continuous improvement. When employees are allowed to fully participate in the selection, analysis and solution of safety and health problems in the workplace, management will need to provide organizational support and specific training to facilitate the problem-solving efforts of team, circle or committee members.

It is important to note that final decision-making authority rests, as always, with management. Management's authority, responsibility and liability are neither delegated to nor appropriated by the safety committee or any employee team actively involved in the safety and health program. The intent of employee involvement is to inform management's decisions in a manner that benefits all members of the corporate body.

Team Concepts

The joint safety and health committee is an established vehicle for implementing employee participation. However, as new operational structures emerge internationally, new avenues are opening for employee involvement. The team concepts that are driving competition worldwide can be applied to both traditional and emerging structures to improve safety and health performance.

We look briefly at some of the team options. However, no single structure is ideal. The organization of any team must suit the culture of the company it serves. Yet, all of the team structures we mention have one common characteristic: they are goal oriented. The purpose of each is to facilitate the solution of problems in the workplace. In the balance of this section, we focus on how management can apply basic team concepts to develop and support an employee team that is oriented toward the resolution of safety-and-health problems, regardless of what form that team takes.

Options: Self-directed work teams, circles, task forces

Many companies have made the transition to team-oriented operational structures in order to streamline and improve production, quality and competitive stance. Business units such as *self-directed work teams* and *focus factories* are based on:

- the perceived value of line-level empirical knowledge

- empowering employees to participate in an on-going decision-making process

- the integration of all aspects of the job—productivity, quality, human performance and safety and health—into a cohesive, team-managed process

Those companies that have successfully implemented such work teams have opened a natural pathway for involving employees in the safety and health program; safety and health become daily considerations—of equal priority with productivity and quality—integrated into the overall process. (It should be noted that a team-oriented company may still need to have a committee structure in place in order to meet regulatory and/or contract stipulations regarding employee involvement.)

Still other organizations have adapted the "quality circle" concept to safety and health. A *safety circle* is similar to a safety and health committee in several ways:

- The circle is organized specifically to address safety and health issues.

- Circle members may perform diverse jobs and functions within the organization.

- A network of circles may serve the complex needs of a large organization.

- The circle meets on a periodic, scheduled basis to review activities and issues.

The focus of the safety circle, however, is more akin to that of a *safety committee task force:* the circle is organized and trained to select, analyze and recommend solutions to specific problems that are causing, or have the potential to cause, losses in the workplace. Thus the circle, like operational team structures, has a built-in orientation toward results. (Again, the circle concept may need to be adapted, or supplemented by a committee structure, to meet legal and/or contract requirements.)

Any employee team, regardless of its specific structure, will require ongoing support and guidance. In the remainder of this section we look at the role of management and staff professionals in relationship to employee teams, then examine the crucial issues that management and professionals must resolve as they guide the team toward continuous improvement.

Organizational Roles

As we will see, organizational roles shift somewhat in relationship to a focused, problem-solving team, whether that team is a committee, committee subgroup, operations team or safety circle. Management and safety/occupational health professionals retain responsibility and accountability for the direction of the overall safety and health program, but they also become facilitators, supporting the growth of the team's abilities and responsibilities. Their responsibilities include, but are not limited to, those listed below.

The safety or occupational health professional:

- plans, schedules and administers the team's training
- assists the team in selecting appropriate safety and health problems to tackle
- observes and coaches team efforts
- provides technical advice to the team
- maintains primary accountability for oversight of the safety and health program

Management:

- observes and leads by example
- remains visible in the safety and health process
- commits resources
- facilitates safety and health changes
- monitors and recognizes team performance
- has primary responsibility and accountability for carrying out the established safety and health program

Tenure of Team Members

The scope of the team's authority, makeup, training, tenure and the focus of its responsibilities should be established in writing when the team is formed. This "charter" defines the team's role and focuses its activities. Moreover, decisions regarding training and tenure will be largely determined by the extent of the team's responsibilities.

The company's commitment of time and resources to the training program can be significant. That investment alone is a strong argument in favor of lengthy tenure for team members, particularly on those teams charged with problem-solving responsibilities. Management cannot expect a return on its investment in a problem-solving team—the ability of a team to efficiently address and expedite the solution to problems—in a matter of weeks, or even a few months. Stable membership also ensures that the problem-solving team has time to adjust to its unique composition of personalities and talents. The tenure of employees representing bargaining groups may be dictated by a union contract.

Training the team

Once the scope, function, and tenure of the team has been established, all team members should be trained in team procedures and in the technical aspects of their responsibilities.

Procedures should be established at the same time that the policy statement or charter defining the team's mission is formulated. Procedures may be reworked or refined as team responsibilities change or grow; however, all new members should become familiar with current forms of conduct at the outset of their tenure.

Technical training should enable team members to knowledgeably execute all of their assigned functions. Because the possible range of team activities is so great, no set of technical training topics is applicable across the board. The responsibilities and activities assigned to the team will need to be analyzed to determine what technical training is necessary. The choices in this area of training include, but are not limited to, the functions listed in Table 7-1.

Technical skills training should be administered by safety and/or occupational health professionals and updated or reaffirmed on a scheduled basis, as special needs arise, or when committee membership changes.

TABLE 7 - 1. TRAINING REQUIREMENTS

Committee Function	Required Training
Hazard identification	Conducting safety and health inspections
Hazard analysis	Job safety analysis
Workplace design	Basic ergonomics; life safety and fire codes; material handling and storage; electrical safety
Injury/illness/incident investigation and control	Investigation procedures; preventable multiple causation; interview techniques
Emergency response	First aid/CPR; fire protection; rescue facility evacuation and shutdown

Those teams further charged with the selection, analysis, and solution of specific safety and health problems will require additional training that addresses the problem-solving process. Procedural and technical knowledge contributes to, but does not produce solutions and results; there are tried and proven techniques that help to analyze and ultimately resolve a problem. Moreover, problem solution is not a straight-line process; it is a circular model of continuous review, adjustment, and improvement. The problem-solving team's training is, therefore, incomplete if it does not address the techniques and dynamics of the continuous improvement process itself. Specifically, this training should include:

- enlistment of management commitment and involvement

- identification, selection, research and analysis of issues/problems

- establishment and communication of goals

- development and implementation of action plans and strategies

- review and adjustment of implemented programs and strategies

- establishment of processes/statistical systems for measuring progress

Training may be conducted through lecture and in-class activities (using staff or consulting professionals), through an "extended case study" approach and in-plant activities or through a combination. Ideally, the training program will provide the team with simulated or controlled hands-on experience. For example, an extended case study can combine technical and problem-solving skills by walking participants through the entire problem-solving sequence under the guidance of instructors.

This approach not only meets the adult learner's need to learn through experience, but prepares the team for the next step: the selection and resolution of an actual safety and health problem in the facility.

Selecting problems and measuring results

Management and staff safety and health professionals assist the team in selecting the problems it will tackle in the workplace. The first few problems that the team takes on are key to building team confidence. For this reason, initial problems should be relatively simple and quickly solved, and their solutions should have observable, measurable results. For example, the team might initiate a cleanup and develop a routine inspection program for an area of operations where relatively minor incidents—cuts, abrasions, trips, minor equipment damage—are occurring as a result of poor housekeeping.

As the team matures, it will begin to select its own problems, and those problems will become more complex and more challenging. Management and safety and health professionals continue to oversee the team's work and retain approval rights for problem selection to ensure that the team's activities are within the scope of its authority and abilities.

Furthermore, the team's focus on results must be maintained. In this respect, they are supported by assistance in selecting projects with specific and demonstrable links between team efforts and safety and health payoffs—both short-term and long-term. Short-term payoffs (for example, the cleaned-up worksite in the housekeeping project above) keep the team focused until the project is completed (development of inspection procedures) and long-term results can be measured (reduction of minor incidents). The team must be provided with a means for clearly quantifying the results of each of its projects—incident statistics, insurance costs, safety and health costs per employee, etc.

How do we further guide the team through the continuous improvement process of constantly reviewing and adjusting team efforts? The primary goal, in this respect, is to maintain the team's orientation toward results. To accomplish this, they must:

- recognize and build on successes
- examine, admit to and learn from failures
- find new areas for improvement
- be cohesive by limiting member turnover
- be focused, completing each task before moving to new challenges
- remain visibly and actively committed

Joint Safety and Health Committees

Joint safety and health committees can take many forms. Each committee will reflect the existing corporate structure and culture and the degree of management's commitment to employee participation. Large organizations can be served by a network of committees, each designed to meet the specific needs of the organizational level or the facility in which it operates.

Committee organization, procedures, functions and authority are further influenced by contract negotiations with organized labor. However, safety committees are formed in both nonunion and union facilities.

Organization

The composition of a joint safety and health committee is such that all organizational levels (management, supervision and employees) are represented. There is no ideal committee size; this will vary with the size and complexity of the corporation or facility. The committee must be small enough to function smoothly; however, since broad representation fosters more complete communication and mutual understanding, an effort should be made to represent a variety of shifts, functions (production, engineering, maintenance, human resources, purchasing, etc.), and other areas of operations.

Employee representation should be at least equal to management representation. Such equality can help to promote the open exchange of information and opinions by assuring employee members that their voice is a prominent one. While management representatives may be appointed, employee representatives should be either elected by their peers or selected from a volunteer pool. Committee membership can be rotated periodically to admit fresh points of view and maximize the number of individuals involved; however, only employees who are truly interested in working on the committee should be members of the committee. No employee should be forced to serve by management's appointment. Union contracts may dictate who the representatives are through elections or appointment by union officials.

The safety committee is usually chaired by a senior manager; however, there is a trend in labor contracts toward requiring co-chairs—a labor representative and a management representative sharing equally in committee oversight. The chairperson(s) oversees all committee activities, including the development of programs and recommendations for establishment of policy.

Staff safety professionals also participate in committee meetings and activities, acting as consultants to the group, guiding and facilitating its efforts whenever necessary. Individuals (coordinators) or subgroups (task forces) of the committee are sometimes appointed in large facilities to work more closely with the safety professional in coordinating specific committee activities or functions (e.g., training, emergency response, injury/illness/incident investigation). Coordinators and/or task forces report directly to the committee on the progress of their activities.

Scope and focus

The scope of authority granted to any given safety committee is determined by management and/or by union contract. A safety committee may be limited to a few specific activities, or it may be the primary body for maintaining safety awareness, motivation and hazard control within a facility. The committee, or a committee task force, may be assigned problem-solving responsibilities (see Team Concepts, above). In any case, the safety committee's scope of authority and range of responsibilities must be clearly defined in its authorizing charter.

The overall mission and specific goals of the safety committee should be expressed in terms of safety and health improvements to the workplace, thus orienting the committee toward the results to be attained. When the committee can point to specific safety and health results it has achieved in the course of its activities, the value of those activities, as perceived by the corporate community at large, is elevated. Committees that focus on and achieve results are far more likely to be successful in enlisting the cooperation of employees outside the committee.

Once committee objectives have been established and communicated, committee functions relevant to those goals must be determined. Those functions may include participation in and/or oversight of:

- determination and communication of safety objectives, policies and standards
- personal protective equipment programs
- safety inspections and self-audits
- investigations of loss-producing events
- job safety analysis
- development and evaluation of safety and health training programs
- emergency response drills
- workstation design
- motivation programs

Committee responsibilities should stay clearly within the safety and health domain and not diverge into management issues. For example, while committee members may be trained to conduct in-depth incident investigations, asking them to also counsel incident repeaters is clearly inappropriate. This is a behavioral issue that should be addressed by personnel trained to do so, such as human resources staff. Charging the safety committee to address matters outside its proper focus is likely to be unsuccessful at best, divisive and counterproductive at worst.

Once the authority and appropriate activities of the committee are established, these operational issues can be addressed:

- appropriate training for committee members (see Team Concepts above)
- where and how often the committee will meet
- reporting procedures
- distribution of responsibilities among team members
- amount of payment to be given hourly and non-exempt salaried employees for participating in committee activities (training time, meeting time, administrative work, etc.)

Meetings

The committee should meet at least monthly to review its activities, the development of programs and any special safety and health issues that have arisen. Problem-solving task forces may meet independently and more frequently. The committee chairman or task force leader should plan the time, place and agenda well in advance. All defined areas of responsibility should be reviewed during these meetings. By adhering to a clear agenda, leaders can maintain control of meetings so that they do not degenerate into gripe sessions or discussions of unrelated side issues.

While most meetings will be convened only for members of the committee, there may be times when it is necessary for other individuals or operational groups to attend in order to discuss specific issues. For example, if incident investigation is a responsibility of the committee, investigation findings should be shared with managers, supervisors and employees who may be affected by any new procedures implemented to prevent repetition of a loss-producing event. These meetings, too, should be well planned, with an agenda circulated in advance to those who will attend so that they may prepare themselves.

Communication

A primary function of many safety and health committees is to foster communication on safety and health issues among all employees. To fulfill this function, the committee should generate reports on its activities to its entire constituency. It may also establish a task force to develop and disseminate safety and health awareness and maintain communications.

By communicating to management, the committee advises management of its activities and of hazards identified, corrections made, and results achieved in the course of those activities. Management should receive copies of the minutes of all meetings, as well as periodic progress reports on committee activities.

By reporting to employees, on the other hand, the committee helps to maintain safety and health awareness throughout the organization. This form of communication will also promote acceptance of safety and health programs by demonstrating the commitment and involvement of both management and fellow employees. Employee communications can be less formal than those to management. Reports can be included in corporate newsletters/magazines, posted on bulletin boards, or circulated in memo form. Committee-sponsored employee safety meetings on pertinent topics also contribute to safety communication, awareness and motivation in the facility.

Union participation

Organized labor unions have always had strong ties to worldwide efforts to foster safer working conditions for all workers. Union activities are not limited to lobbying governments to protect the well-being of workers; labor leaders recognize the importance of workers taking an active role in resolving the safety and health problems they face in the workplace. Safety and health are also significant considerations during contract negotiations. (In the United States, approximately 90% of union contracts covering manufacturing workers contain safety and health language.)

The commitment of organized labor to worker safety and employee involvement brings a special point of view to the safety committees on which union members serve. Labor may also negotiate specific stipulations regarding membership in, organization of and payment of labor members for time spent on committee activities.

While these are legitimate concerns of labor, we must note at this point that occasionally organized labor will regard the formation of a union-participation committee as an opportunity to control decision making. Such an attitude can create a serious organizational problem and set up the committee for discord and possible failure. Negotiation and the committee charter should clearly establish that final authority and responsibility for safety and health decisions rest with management and staff professionals.

There are three basic types of union-participation safety and health committees, each with its own organizational and procedural nuances.

Joint union-management committees are formed by labor contract to foster labor-management communication on safety and health in the workplace. The joint committee provides labor and management an opportunity to work together to solve safety and health problems without work stoppages or the intervention of regulatory agencies.

Freedom of expression without fear of reprisal is of primary concern on joint committees; for this reason, equal labor-management representation is often established by labor contract. Contract provisions can also include specific language that determines committee leadership; union and management representatives may alternate terms chairing the committee, or a labor member and management member may serve as co-chairs. Contracts may also specify the method for selection of labor committee members. Whether that method is election or selection from a pool of volunteers, selection of labor representatives is made by other union members, not by management.

Independent union committees are union-only safety committees, organized and operated solely by union members commonly used as a means of addressing the safety and health concerns of one or more unions operating in the workplace. Such a committee operates completely independently of management and may be created at any time, regardless of contract language; its members are elected or appointed according to a union's by-laws. The independent union committee is also a separate entity from any existing joint committee. However, where both independent and joint committees exist in a single workplace, there is often cross-representation; that is, one or more members of the independent committee may also serve on the joint committee.

The independent committee's autonomy allows for union evaluation of the joint committee. Labor also has an opportunity to set its own priorities and procedures for addressing workplace hazards. Labor representatives may then bring these preferences to the joint committee table. Further, if the joint committee is disbanded for any reason, labor still has an organization in place for addressing safety and health concerns.

The committee's procedures, activities and scope of authority are determined by the union and committee members; however, certain practices are fairly standard among independent committees. For example, the committee will commonly involve itself in contract negotiations to ensure that safety and health issues are covered knowledgeably during the negotiation process. The committee may also meet regularly with the union grievance committee, and together these two groups establish procedures for handling safety and health-related grievances.

Multiple-union mutual committees are sometimes used in special situations when more than one organized labor group is represented at the facility or at a special project site (e.g., construction sites). A mutual committee is formed to address the safety and health issues or specific workplace hazards common to all workers on-site. Membership on the committee includes representatives from each union and can also include cross-representation from other safety committees (independent or joint committees) organized at the facility or site.

Individual Efforts

Every employee is both entitled to and responsible for safety and health in the workplace regardless of whether or not the individual is a member of a committee or team with safety and health responsibilities. Management should support individual efforts by providing clear guidelines, facilitating employee input and acknowledging individual achievements.

Responsibility and accountability

A thorough safety and health program should begin with definition and assignment of safety and health responsibility and accountability for all levels of management and all employees. This establishes what is expected of both management and employees in terms of their roles in the safety and health program; it is the first step in enlisting individual involvement. The employee's basic responsibilities should include:

- awareness of and compliance with all company safety and health requirements (practices and procedures)

- awareness of and compliance with emergency procedures

- commitment to ask for help when unsure of how to perform any task safely

- commitment to report unsafe practices and hazardous work conditions and procedures

Management underpins employee responsibility by also establishing accountability for safety and health. Each employee's contribution to workplace safety should be considered in the assessment of his or her overall job performance.

Soliciting individual opinions, suggestions and input

Everyone has something to contribute to the improvement of safety and health in the workplace. Management and staff professionals should acknowledge this by establishing systems that elicit individual input on an ongoing basis. An *employee suggestion system* that allows employees to contribute their suggestions and opinions in writing via an established procedure is a beginning. Yet the suggestion system cannot stand alone. Management must buttress this formal process by constantly providing employees with opportunities to participate in the protection of their own well-being.

Safety contacts are commonly initiated after job safety observations or as part of a job safety analysis (JSA) process. (See Element 1.) This type of contact is highly individual in nature, involving a one-on-one safety-related meeting or discussion between supervisor and employee. After observing the employee at work, the supervisor takes the opportunity to both recognize and reinforce safe job performance, and to offer constructive criticism and further instruction as necessary. The employee, on the other hand, is given the opportunity to voice opinions regarding his or her own performance and company safety and health rules, procedures and programs in a forum where he or she is assured of being heard.

Job Safety Analyses (JSAs) formally allow employees to participate in identifying hazards and unsafe practices in the workplace and modify work methods to prevent injury, illness and incidents and improve productivity and product quality. The JSA process encourages safe work practices on a personal level by a process that relies on their expertise and knowledge about each job and its related tasks. When used as a tool for continuous improvement, the JSA facilitates better communication between line employees, supervisors and senior managers.

Safety and health meetings are most often thought of as a means of training and disseminating safety and health information to employees, but they can also be a forum for soliciting employee input. The downfall of many safety meetings is that they are regarded as obligatory, both by the presenter and the audience. Just holding a safety meeting does not guarantee that safety and health are addressed in a manner that is meaningful to employees. The meeting should be well-planned around a topic that is truly relevant to the well-being of those attending. It should be presented in an organized manner by a supervisor, team member, staff member or consulting professional who is well prepared and well versed in the discussion topic. Finally, plenty of time should be set aside at the conclusion of the presentation for feedback and questions from the audience. A detailed agenda, circulated in advance to the target audience, allows those attending to prepare themselves to participate.

Perception surveys are a means of giving all employees a voice in the direction of the safety and health program. The corporate safety and health program cannot be truly effective unless it is perceived as having value, and acted on accordingly, by employees. These surveys quantify the attitudes that influence acceptance and safe job performance. A company-wide or facility-wide perception survey can pinpoint program inadequacies and credibility gaps in management's commitment to safety. Moreover, because the survey is anonymous and administered to all levels, all employees have an equal voice—even those who might be unable or unwilling to voice dissatisfaction in other circumstances. Results of the survey must be made known to all participants in a timely manner. (More detailed information on perception surveys is provided in Element 14.)

Employee recognition

Half of the continuous improvement process is a matter of correcting weaknesses; the other half is a matter of building on strengths. Employees who perform their work safely and become involved in the company safety and health effort are definitely in the latter category. The value of such performance is reinforced when it is formally recognized by management.

Individual employee performance appraisals of some companies require an assessment of the individual's safety and health contributions and performance. Inasmuch as performance appraisals are tied to financial reward and performance possibilities, employee participation is recognized as valuable to the company.

We have seen that recognition of safe job performance can and should be ongoing and personal through a system of safety contacts. Yet, there will be times that management will wish to publicly recognize individual and group efforts in the area of safety and health. Certainly, all of the following contributions deserve some form of recognition:

- implemented suggestions or recommendations
- reduction of safety- and health-related losses
- achievement of significant loss-free production hours
- demonstrated high level of safety awareness/activity

Recognition may be as simple as posting the name and picture of an individual who has made a good suggestion on a bulletin board or in a newsletter or company magazine, along with a description of the suggestion. Many companies also employ more systematic methods of recognition—for example, issuing certificates or plaques at annual safety awards ceremonies. Management may chose to participate in the structured award programs sponsored annually by nationally recognized organizations, such as the National Safety Council or OSHA.

All such actions have value; the mere fact of recognition reinforces safe job performance and safety and health awareness. But recognition must also be graduated, its breadth and value increasing with the significance of the contribution or achievement. Truly milestone achievements deserve more than plaques and publicity. Financial rewards are sometimes tied to recognition, but financial incentives are not always necessary when management's action is evidence of its appreciation.

For example, an Iowa (U.S.) firm implemented an employee involvement program that took the company from being a poor safety performer to "best in class" (and two Awards of Honor from the National Safety Council) in five years. When one of its facilities—a 300-employee manufacturing plant—completed a year of record production with only a few hundred dollars in safety-related losses, the company's top executives flew hundreds of miles to formally and personally recognize the achievement. Management recognition of this magnitude is not uncommon in organizations that are truly committed to safety and health.

Employee Involvement Review

The following worksheet suggests some of the questions management must answer in order to assess the level of its own commitment to employee participation and to establish the baseline status of current employee involvement systems. These issues are guidelines; as you work through them, you will want to consider employee involvement issues specific to your company's needs, culture and structure.

TABLE 7 - 2. EMPLOYEE INVOLVEMENT REVIEW

Issues/Questions	In Place Yes	No	Partially	Action Plan (if answer is "no" or Partially")
7.1 Are committees/teams used to foster employee involvement in safety and health?				
7.2 Are committees/teams formally chartered with objectives, functions, authority and membership/leader selection processes established in writing?				
7.3 Is representation diverse, including a variety of shifts, functions and employee levels?				
7.4 Is a program established for training all members in procedures, problem-solving and technical issues?				
7.5 Is technical training administered by professionals and appropriate to the full range of the group's functions?				
7.6 Does management require, review and respond to formal reports on committee/team meetings, activities and recommendations?				

TABLE 7 - 2. EMPLOYEE INVOLVEMENT REVIEW Continued

| Issues/Questions | In Place | | | Action Plan |
	Yes	No	Partially	(if answer is "no" or "Partially")
7.7 Have resources been committed to meet team/committee needs?				
7.8 Does the employee involvement program meet regulatory require-ments and contract stipulations?				
7.9 Have safety and health responsibility and accountability been defined for all employees and management?				
7.10 Are individual employees given opportunities to voice opinions/concerns (meetings, surveys, suggestion system, safety and health contacts, JSAs, etc.)?				
7.11 Does management give formal recognition to outstanding individual and group contributions to safety and health?				

References

Books

Bird FE, Germain GL. *Practical Loss Control Leadership.* Loganville, GA: International Loss Control Institute, 1990.

National Safety Council. *Accident Prevention Manual for Business & Industry: Administration & Programs,* 10th ed. Itasca, IL: NSC, 1992.

National Safety Council. *Protecting Workers' Lives,* 2nd ed. Itasca, IL: NSC, 1992.

Orsburn J, Moran L, Musselwhite E, et al. *Self-Directed Work Teams: The New American Challenge.* Homewood, IL: Business One Irwin, 1990.

Articles

Etter IB. Safety committees: the eyes and ears of a good safety program. *Safety & Health,* November 1993.

Everly M. Are you ready for 1993? *Health and Safety at Work* (England), January 1993.

Kaletta JP. Re-engineering the safety process. *Managing the Process* (a newsletter about safety, health and environmental consulting). National Safety Council, December 1993.

Norris E. Joint safety committees: labor and management say 'we do.' *Safety & Health,* November 1993.

Planek T., Fearn K. Reevaluating occupational safety priorities: 1967 to 1992. *Professional Safety,* October 1993.

Schaffer R., Thomson H. Successful change programs begin with results. *Harvard Business Review,* January-February 1992.

Packaged Training Programs

National Safety Council. Agenda 2000® Safety Health Environment Program. Itasca, IL: NSC, 1992.

Petersen D. The Dan Petersen Safety Management Series. Safety Training Systems, 1990.

Surveys

Planek T., Kolosh, K. Survey of Employee Participation in Safety and Health. Itasca, IL: National Safety Council, 1993.

Government Publications

U.S. General Accounting Office. *Occupational Safety and Health. Differences Between Program in the United States and Canada,* GAO/HRD-94-15FS. Washington, DC: U.S. GAO, December 1993.

Safety Representatives and Safety Committees Regulations 1977. London, England: Health and Safety Commission Executive, 1977.

Award Programs

Motivation: Safety Programs Targeted to Recognize Individuals and Organizations. Itasca, IL: National Safety Council, 1993.

Occupational Safety and Health Administration. Voluntary Protection Programs. *Federal Register,* vol. 53, no. 133. Washington, D.C.: U.S. GPO, July 12, 1988.

EXECUTIVE SUMMARY — ELEMENT 8

Motivation involves moving people to action that supports or achieves desired goals. In occupational safety and health, motivation increases the awareness, interest and willingness of employees to act in ways that increase their personal safety and that of co-workers, and that support an organization's stated goals and objectives.

Motivation aims primarily at changing behavior and attitudes and is generally defined by three factors: direction of behavior, intensity of action and persistence of effort.

Among the many approaches that companies have used to motivate employees to improve safety and health performance, two general ones have had considerable influence. One, the organization behavior management (OBM) model, is tied directly to the use of reinforcement and feedback to modify behavior. The other, the total quality management (TQM) model, flows from attitude adjustment methods used to achieve quality improvement goals in industry.

The ultimate success of a motivational model in changing employee attitudes and behavior depends on visible management leadership. In addition, the motivational techniques used should support the mainline safety and health management system, not take its place. Similarly, evaluation of the worth of these techniques should be measured in terms of how well they achieve their support roles, such as maintaining employees' interest in their own safety, rather than by their effect on injury rates. Three specific motivational techniques are discussed: communications, incentives/awards/recognition and employee surveys.

Element **8**

■ ■ ■ ■ ■ ■ ■ ■ ■ ■ ■ ■ ■

MOTIVATION, BEHAVIOR AND ATTITUDES

In a study that compared occupational safety priorities in the '90s with those of the '60s, Planek and Fearn (1993) found that safety professionals are now more concerned with managing the human element of the safety and health system than they were 25 years ago. In addition, as a group, safety professionals today are in less agreement about what they should do to address the human element than they were in the '60s.

Many companies are moving away from traditional approaches to managing employee safety and health. These approaches exhibited such characteristics as top/down communication, minimal employee participation and a dependence on discipline to influence safety behavior. The problems of motivating employees, changing attitudes and controlling behavior continue to resist uniform, simple solutions.

The term *motivation* refers to a theoretical concept that has been the subject of a great deal of research. Alternative theories relate to how and why people are "motivated" either to adopt new behaviors or to change old ones. Questions exist involving the relationship between attitudes and behavior. Must attitude change come before behavior change? Can behavior change exist without attitude change? Does attitude change predict behavior change? Does behavior change cause attitude change?

Answers to these questions are uncertain. The research and theoretical literature in psychology contains proponents on every side of these issues. There are those who insist that motivation is best achieved by focusing on external behavior change, while others believe that internal attitude or cognitive change must occur.

These concepts have been carried over into the occupational safety and health field, and concept variations have been applied to employee management, training, communication and control techniques. Currently, two models appear to be of particular interest to safety professionals. One involves an emphasis on the use of behavior modification to improve safety performance. The other involves the use of attitude modification and behavioral concepts to modify safety processes. However, employee motivation is the goal of both of these models.

In everyday language, the word *motivation* refers to a variety of external and internal "pushes" and "pulls" that help to explain a person's actions. It is commonplace to hear safety professionals discuss the need to "motivate" management to support the safety and health program, or "motivate" employees to wear safety glasses or to follow safe job procedures. What they are really seeking are ways to change or reactivate the behaviors and attitudes of people to meet defined safety goals.

Motivation is closely tied to learning. In fact, the term itself originated in the context of learning theory development. Weiss (1990) defines learning as a relatively permanent change in knowledge or skill produced by experience.

Learning how to avoid hazardous situations or prevent them from occurring is a process that begins in childhood. In workplace situations, training is the fundamental means of acquiring knowledge, building skills and developing an understanding of rules.

Even though learning occurs, however, it may not be reflected in employee behavior without the appropriate motivation. The methods covered in this chapter examine conditions that are necessary to motivate safe behavior and how they can be introduced and supported within an organization's safety and health program.

The discussion begins with a definition of motivation and its general characteristics. It then examines two approaches or models that can be used to motivate employees, one focusing on behavior and the other on attitudes. Finally, three techniques intended to increase employee interest in and acceptance of improved safety and health performance are presented.

Definition of Motivation

Kanfer (1990) indicates that motivation involves three variables:

- *Direction of behavior* in terms of the performance of actions that accomplish defined objectives

- *Intensity of action* in terms of the amount of personal attention and thought given to the performance of goal-oriented actions

- *Persistence of effort* so that desired performance lasts over time

Direction of behavior requires two supporting actions. First, the behaviors to be achieved (or output to be obtained) must be specified. Second, employees must clearly understand how to achieve the desired objective(s).

Safety and health objectives can be defined very narrowly in terms of specific behaviors, or broadly in terms of process improvements. Once objectives have been set, employees must receive the knowledge necessary to achieve them. Unless these two elements are present, motivational efforts are futile.

Intensity of action means that employees integrate safety and health objectives into their job assignments with the same degree of mental and emotional effort that they expend for other work objectives. It also implies that employees may have to be willing to spend extra time to incorporate safety and health practices into their routine work patterns and, if necessary, accept the potentially bothersome aspects of some new behaviors that may be required.

To ensure that employees are seriously involved, the reinforcement of appropriate behaviors and/or performance levels should be as strong as possible. Also, communication of performance results to employees is critical to the change process both to demonstrate achievement and to emphasize its importance.

Persistence of effort relates directly to the nurturing and maturing of the attitudes or action tendencies that support improved safety and health performance throughout the organization. For this continuity of purpose to occur, both employees and management must be committed. Employees must be willing to modify personal behavior in accordance with company safety goals and objectives. Management must be visibly committed and active in its support for employee safety and health.

Specification of safety objectives or goals

Conard (1983) and Cohen (1987) have suggested several broad classes of behavioral actions that have worksite hazard control implications. The majority focus on prevention, but some deal with the mitigation of unwanted effects during and after incident occurrence.

In the area of prevention, critical behaviors include:

- proper use and operation of equipment to maximize safe performance
- adherence to work procedures that maximize safe performance
- avoidance of actions that increase risk of injury or illness
- recognition of physical and process-related hazards
- observance of good housekeeping, maintenance and personal hygiene practices

With respect to injury/illness/incident mitigation, critical behaviors include:

- proper and consistent use of personal protective equipment and other controls
- recognition of illness-related symptoms
- proper response(s) to emergency situations

In each of these classes, the specific behaviors to be identified and practiced or avoided vary from company to company. Company operating policies, rules and procedures normally address general safety practices. OSHA and related laws specify selected areas of compliance. The company's "way of doing things," bolstered by group norms, also tends to influence safety priorities.

Often, however, the information from these sources is not sufficiently specific to cover the complete array of tasks that must be performed at the most basic operational levels. Furthermore, policies, rules and regulatory standards seldom, by themselves, carry the motivational impact necessary to affect safe job performance on a continuing basis. Additional understanding of workplace safety needs and improvement opportunities can come from injury/illness/incident investigations as well as through periodic inspections and audits. These procedures frequently pinpoint safety deficiencies in a concrete way and with an immediacy that directly influences employees to improve their performance.

To supplement investigations, inspections and audits and add considerably to their potential for stimulating safe behavior, employee involvement in the formulation of safety needs is also advisable. Job safety analysis, which allows employees to participate in the identification of hazards and means for their elimination, lays an important foundation for behavior change. This type of participation should be reinforced and continued through an open communication system that welcomes safety discussion on the part of employees, and offers a means for action in response to suggestions and corrective action when problems or hazards are reported. In this regard, the use of employee safety program perception and attitude assessments can play a significant role both in specifying process safety priorities and in enhancing employee morale. The role of surveys as a motivational stimulus to improved performance is detailed later in this chapter.

Once safety improvement objectives are specified, employees must learn how to attain them. Training or retraining of employees is often a necessary step at this juncture of the improvement process and lays the groundwork for immediate positive results. With the proper thrust and scope, training in hazard identification and other skills can also develop an employee's capacity to make knowledgeable contributions to improved job safety performance.

Reinforcement of desired behaviors

Once safety objectives are defined and the behaviors necessary to attain them are known, they must become part of the job performance action pattern. To achieve this, employees must initially pay attention to job safety requirements and put what they have learned into practice. This frequently means that habitual and comfortable behaviors must be eliminated or altered, while behaviors that are unfamiliar and possibly unsettling are substituted.

If employees are involved in specifying safety and health improvement objectives and receive adequate training, the reinforcement of behavior change has already begun. (Reinforcement in this context refers to anything that encourages the repetition of a behavior.)

Two important characteristics influence the effectiveness of reinforcement. First, it is generally agreed that positive reinforcement—such as personal recognition or performance awards, which focus on increasing the occurrence of desired behaviors—is more efficient in achieving higher levels of safety performance than forms of disciplinary action focused on eliminating unwanted behaviors. Secondly, the closer in time a reinforcement is associated with a behavior, the stronger its effect.

Both of these principles flow from learning theories that were developed largely on the basis of animal behavior studies. Principles derived from these studies have been used as a basis for explaining how learning occurs in humans. These studies have also led to the development of a variety of "need" and "drive" theories about why people behave as they do. Based on these theories, it can be observed that timely, positive reinforcement of specific behaviors and action patterns, and general feedback about performance that has produced the desired result(s) or achieved the intended objective(s), are considered essential features of the learning and motivation process.

Group feedback can create a very positive atmosphere for behavior change. When a work group accepts common safety improvement objectives, its members tend to reinforce one another's behaviors. To make this happen, feedback at the group level should be maintained. Whether or not positive change is achieved, feedback provides momentum for future accomplishment.

Group feedback requires objective evaluation or measurement of progress. The establishment of a measurement system begins with the definition of the specified safety and health objectives so that they can be observed. Observation can be direct when specific behaviors are involved and can take the form of counting the occurrences of unsafe behaviors or their by-products. To observe progress toward achieving broadly defined process improvement goals, surveys or other performance indicators may be required. These examine such factors as the current level of employee involvement in safety and health activities and the effectiveness of safety and health management system processes.

Whatever measurements are used, feedback at the group level requires the collection of baseline data and a commitment to continue the measurement process. Feedback maintains individual interest in and attention to the desired safety objectives. It also helps to make the newly elicited safety action patterns part of a work group's job performance norm.

Attainment of commitment and involvement

Attainment of permanent performance improvement is a product of employee and management commitment and involvement. Employee acceptance must occur and management leadership must be visible.

When behaviors are repeated and reinforced, the foundation has been laid for personal acceptance to occur. In other words, employees are willing to take the responsibility for paying attention to the behavior or process changes necessary to achieve specified safety and health objectives until they become part of their habitual action patterns.

A change in work habits is not attained overnight. Rather, it takes time to accomplish and must have continuous management support. Employees must perceive that management at all levels is behind the objectives of the safety and health program and supports the methods chosen to achieve them. If at all possible, the techniques used to motivate employees should blend with an organization's culture. They should not be viewed as "special" or outside the management mainstream, but rather as part and parcel of the motivational methods that are used to achieve high levels of production and quality.

When this mesh is present, the likelihood that safety and health needs will be accommodated within the normal business function is high and, therefore, the potential for permanent improvement is increased. When motivation and behavior change techniques do not fit in with a company's management style or are looked upon as non-mainstream activities, even though they receive considerable initial attention, they are unlikely to become permanent.

Description of Motivation Models

Among the many models that can be used to motivate employees to improve safety and health performance, two have had considerable acceptance. One, the organization behavior management (OBM) model, is tied directly to the use of reinforcement and feedback to modify behavior. The other, the total quality management (TQM) model, flows from attitude adjustment methods used to achieve quality improvement goals in industry.

As shown in Table 8-1, both management approaches are responsive to the motivational variables and supporting actions that have been described. The models vary, however, on the safety emphasis used to motivate employees. As a result, they differ in terms of their efficiency in accomplishing the requirements of the three motivational variables.

TABLE 8 - 1. COMPARISON OF OBM VS. TQM APPROACHES TO EMPLOYEE MOTIVATION

Motivational Variable	Supporting Action	Safety Emphasis OBM Model	Safety Emphasis TQM Model
Direction of Behavior	Specify Objectives Provide Training	Behavior Behavior Training	Attitudes/Behavior Process Education
Intensity of Action	Give Reinforcement Maintain Feedback	Behavior Occurrence Behavior Data	Process Improvement Operating Indicators
Persistence of Effort	Commit Employee Commit Management	Behavior Change Style Change	Continuous Improvement Cultural Change

The theoretical orientation of the models differs with regard to the specification of safety and health objectives. As Table 8-1 shows, OBM emphasizes external behavior change, while TQM emphasizes internal attitudinal changes as a prerequisite to behavior change. Accordingly, OBM objectives can probably be communicated in a more direct and simple fashion to employees, while TQM principles may be more complex and unfamiliar.

Training provided to employees through OBM and TQM differs as well. OBM training is specific in its coverage of critical behaviors to be changed, while TQM education includes behavioral as well as attitudinal skills development, such as team building and problem solving.

Reinforcement and feedback are provided by both OBM and TQM models, but the observational techniques used in OBM are more formal and specific to the objectives (i.e., specific behavior changes) than are those used in TQM. Also, the reinforcement/feedback schedules used in OBM are more structured than those found in TQM, thus facilitating behavior changes more rapidly.

Employee commitment to improved safety performance on a permanent basis as reflected in both attitude and behavior changes appears more directly attained by TQM than OBM, because of TQM's emphasis on process or root cause improvements. Process changes produced by TQM flow from employee involvement and empowerment as individuals and teams. Employees are much more likely to support change if the objectives to be achieved and the methods used to achieve them are based on their own recommendations rather than imposed by management.

OBM's emphasis on critical behaviors or special cause improvements includes some degree of employee participation in the selection of behaviors to be changed and, possibly, the incentives to be used, but control is maintained through a relatively rigid observation and reinforcement system. As a result, unless the system is continued, the permanence of the behavior change remains questionable.

With regard to management commitment, TQM requires a definite change from the philosophy that employees should be "managed" to conform to existing systems to a viewpoint that processes and systems can be improved or even completely revamped, and that employees are in the best position to know how those processes work and should work. It also calls for creation of a corporate culture that features flexibility and responsiveness to employee needs and trust between labor and management.

The OBM approach does not demand a shift from the traditional management philosophy that seeks to manage employee behavior. It does, however, call for the acceptance of a new management style that focuses on a different and relatively exacting observation system that is not widely used and that requires a relatively substantial amount of time and resources to maintain.

Description of Selected Motivational Techniques

No matter how intrinsically effective a motivational model is in changing employee attitudes and behavior, its ultimate success depends on visible management leadership. This is a prerequisite for any program, whether it is focused on production, product quality or employee safety and health. It is the consistent finding that cuts across all successful safety programs despite their differences. As Cohen and Cleveland (1983), in their study of outstanding National Safety Council member companies, conclude: "No safety program was quite like any other. However, all had one major thing in common: safety in each instance was a real priority in corporate policy and action."

Besides this essential ingredient, there are many other productive motivational techniques that can be used to promote employee safety and health or otherwise influence employees to take "self-protective" action against workplace hazards. These have been reviewed by a number of authors, including Cohen, Smith and Anger (1979), Cohen (1987) and Peters (1991).

It must be emphasized that the role of motivation efforts is to support the mainline safety and health management system, not take its place. Safety and health programs are more likely to succeed when the programs are energized through slogans, performance recognition and discipline in combination with safe and healthful workplace conditions; well-designed tools, equipment and workplace layout; effective maintenance; and appropriate training and supervision.

Similarly, evaluation of the worth of motivation techniques should not be measured by reduction in injuries, property damage or workers' compensation costs. Rather, their effectiveness should be judged in terms of how well they achieve their support roles, such as maintaining employees' interest in their own safety, communicating management's interest in employee safety and health, generating employee involvement in safety activities, increasing morale and reminding employees to take special precautions.

Cohen et al. (1979) point out that these approaches "seek to establish a generalized tendency to act in safe and healthful ways through appropriate attitude change, increased knowledge or heightened awareness." This discussion briefly highlights three of them.

Communication

Communications of various kinds are used to enhance the general effectiveness of any motivational effort. The communication process can be summed up thus: *Who* says *what*, in *which channel*, to *whom* and with what *effect?* Accordingly, communication programs usually involve a source, message, media, target and objectives.

Communications vary in terms of their coverage and impact. Safety posters, banners and other mass media are high in coverage and most effective in increasing general awareness about safety and health issues and in presenting on-the-spot directions or safety reminders. They can also be a useful vehicle for making employees aware of management's general interest in their welfare. As is the case with mass media in general, their impact is lessened when used alone because they provide no opportunity for interaction, further information or response to questions. However, the impact of their message can be increased when combined with opportunities for person-to-person or two-way communication, either through group discussions or individual contacts. Though low in coverage value, these methods can be high in impact and lead to changes in behavior.

Credibility of source is very important in safety and health communications. Bauer (1965) describes two types of credibility:

- Problem solving—based on competence and trust

- Compliance—based on likability and prestige

In this model the problem-solving source is more likely to prompt lasting behavior change than the compliance-based source. In the workplace, supervisor competence in terms of knowledge of the task and the hazards involved as well as in the setting of a good example are seen by Cohen et al. (1979) as important to making supervisors credible sources of safety and health information by employees.

With regard to communication content, the use of fear has been a topic of research and controversy for years. This strategy attempts to change safety and health attitudes about the risks involved in hazardous behaviors by instilling fear in a target audience and then reducing that fear by providing methods to prevent the danger or lower the risk. Workplace examples include personal protective equipment use campaigns, while non-workplace examples include anti-smoking campaigns and seat belt use programs. The main argument against using fear messages is the contention that receivers "block out" or suppress the message.

Based on his review of the research literature, Peters (1991) gives these recommendations for using fear messages:

- The message should attempt to evoke a high (versus low) level of fear.

- The suggested preventive actions should be relatively detailed, specific and presented immediately after the fear response is evoked.

- The preventive actions should be presented in a block, rather than interspersed with information designed to elicit fear.

- The suggested preventive actions must be perceived by the target audience to be effective in preventing danger.

- The source of the communication should have high credibility. Most research suggests the direct supervisor as being the best source for fear messages.

- Person-to-person, two-way communication is more effective than written, one-way communication.

- Increased effectiveness can be achieved by gaining the support of significant others, such as co-workers, supervisors and family.

Finally, safety and health communications should consider the target group(s) at which messages are aimed. For example, research has shown that fear messages are more effective with new employees than with seasoned employees who can use their experiences to discount the message. Additionally, fear messages have been found to be especially effective in influencing employees who are not under direct supervision and are expected to comply with safety regulations on their own.

As an aid to both defining targets and establishing objectives, employee surveys are recommended to assess current levels of safety and health knowledge, attitudes toward safety management programs and practices and compliance with rules and procedures. Such measurements assist in pinpointing education and persuasion priorities and set a baseline for later evaluations of the effectiveness of communication efforts.

Cohen (1987) provides these general guidelines for communications:

- Statistics or risk data has greatest impact if it is workplace- or place-specific.

- Persons in the communications target group should be involved in planning communication content.

- Pilot testing of communication programs is advisable.

Finally, Planek (1969) points out that because of the unknowns involved in the attitude change/behavior change process, evaluations of the success of communications programs should be guided by the following principles:

Observed success in conveying knowledge or changing attitude is not an indicator of behavior change unless further observation of behavior is made.

Awards/Incentives/Recognitions

The use of incentives, awards and recognitions to motivate employees to perform safely is an accepted feature of both OBM and TQM models. In the OBM model, use of incentives to reinforce employee behavior is critical to program success. In TQM, rewards, promotions and other incentives are used to recognize individuals for contributions to process improvement. Also, at the group, team, or company level, special days or other functions are used to celebrate achievement.

Broadly speaking, the use of incentives of any type—including salary increases and promotions—can be viewed as having a positive influence on employee attitudes and behavior. When safety and health is made part of the decision to reward employee performance, these factors take on added significance as important job-related requirements.

Cohen et al. (1979) comment that the use of incentive and award programs is controversial. Given the wide use of incentives and awards of some kind in all phases of social enterprise, one may wonder why this controversy exists. The problems with such programs tend to arise when they are misused or abused. At the organization level, incentive or award programs for employees can be substituted for legitimate safety and health management programs. As has been indicated, motivational techniques support mainline programs but are never a substitute for them. At the employee level, abuse can result in the failure to report an injury or incident for fear that either an individual or work group will not receive an award.

Many companies use incentives and awards as part of their safety and health program on a continuing basis. Certainly, the OBM literature is filled with success stories supporting the use of incentives, and there is a great amount of anecdotal evidence citing the successful use of a wide variety of reward programs.

There is also some evidence presented by Deci (1975) that distinguishes between the effects of rewards that are perceived as "controlling," as can happen in the OBM approach to the reinforcement of safe behaviors, and those that are viewed as "informational," which is the emphasis in the TQM model. Studies that explore these differences (Kanfer, 1990) have found that rewards that recognize personal competence, as occur in TQM, are stronger than those that simply provide positive performance feedback, as is the case in OBM. One explanation for this finding is that employees perceive informational rewards, which recognize achievement and personal competence, to be under their own control rather than "in the hands" of another person who gives or withholds rewards based on the performance being observed. Accordingly, the focus for control of informational rewards is within the employee or intrinsic, as opposed to being outside the employee or extrinsic, as is the case for controlling rewards.

Awards that recognize achievement at the company or corporate level are also worthy of discussion. In the arena of quality alone there are two national awards of note, the President's Award for Quality and Productivity Improvement and the Malcolm Baldrige National Quality Award, both of which have attracted the attention of top U.S. corporations. Similarly, the National Safety Council provides awards for outstanding records in occupational safety and health.

The purpose of these awards is also to recognize achievement and reinforce the actions that led to successful corporate performance at all organizational levels. When these awards are applauded throughout recipient companies, they can be a powerful stimulus for continuous improvement. Indeed, the Council's Occupational Safety/Health Award Program draws applications from more than 6,000 member companies annually.

Here again, however, problems of misuse can occur insidiously in organizations that receive national awards for excellence in safety and health. When management uses attainment of an annual award as the sole criterion of program achievement, two forms of misuse are possible. Management may have a self-satisfied attitude that causes it to ignore or be otherwise unresponsive to safety and health system and performance inadequacies that have not caused lost workdays, injuries or deaths. Or, it may adopt a "win at all costs" posture that generates counterproductive stress and can lead to abuses in reporting or in the proper handling of employee injuries and illnesses. In either of these cases, a national organizational award loses its effectiveness and becomes a hindrance to continuous safety and health improvement.

In summary, the appropriate use of awards, incentives, and recognitions can play an important helping role for organizations that use them wisely. They can, as Cohen et al. (1979) conclude, "add interest to an established hazard control program, which could enhance self-protective actions on the part of the work force."

Employee surveys

Employee surveys in the form of questionnaires and/or interviews are becoming a widely used means of uncovering safety and health management systems strengths and weaknesses. They play a critical role in TQM approaches to employee motivation as a source of information on safety and health needs as well as measures of performance improvement.

Surveys also stimulate employee participation in safety and health. As Planek (1993) points out, "It makes sense to include employees when designing program plans intended to increase their safety and health. When gathered in an objective and representative fashion, candid employee input can provide unique insights about the current status of safety and health and assist the selection of improvement priorities." DeJoy (1986) points out other positive effects of employee participation through surveys, such as heightened employee awareness and interest in safety, and the perception that management is not only interested in employee safety and health but also that it is open to employee input on the subject.

At a minimum, a basic employee survey should consider the following five factors:

- *Management Leadership*—that clearly communicates a safety and health vision supported in words and action.

- *Supervision Involvement*—that reinforces and communicates management's vision through open employee interactions, example, training, control and recognition.

- *Employee Responsibility*—that personally supports company safety/health objectives and adopts the attitudes and action necessary to achieve them.

- *Safety Support Activities*—that generate employee cooperation and action to achieve safety and health objectives, such as a management/nonmanagement safety committee.

- *Safety Support Climate*—that sustains employees' perception that management is completely committed to employee safety and health as a top priority.

Like the other techniques that are discussed in this chapter, the benefits that can be derived from employee surveys depend on how they are used. For example, if survey results are acted on by management, they can greatly enhance employee morale and provide a strong indication that management is serious about employee safety and health. This image can be further enhanced if results are communicated to employees, at least in summary form. If, in contrast, management fails to follow up on findings, the survey activity can prove detrimental to morale and damaging to management's image with regard to employee safety and health.

This situation is particularly critical in organizations whose management style has been traditionally nonparticipative. An employee survey can be an effective way to initiate increased employee participation and to communicate this change in management style to employees. However, if there is no intention to change the prevailing management style, the use of a survey will be seen simply as "window dressing."

The primary reason for conducting an employee survey is to obtain as accurate a picture as possible of how the safety and health management system is operating. Whether or not an organization has open communications, it is frequently difficult to get an objective and balanced view of employee reactions to safety and health programs and activities. Communication barriers, whether personal on the part of individual employees or organizational in nature, can produce unbalanced impressions about program strengths as well as weaknesses.

For this reason, it is necessary to ensure that all employees are given an equal opportunity to participate in a survey. This may be done by including all employees in the activity or by selecting a random sample of employees that truly represents the workplace population. If the former approach is taken, the activity takes on added morale-building value, because all employees are given an opportunity to express their opinion. However, economic considerations may preclude this possibility, particularly in large organizations. In such cases, a random sample of respondents is appropriate if the proper selection techniques are used.

It takes time, effort and resources to conduct an employee survey. Accordingly, management must be clear in how it intends to use survey findings and resolved to do whatever it takes to obtain the most objective and, therefore, most accurate and reliable results possible.

Motivation, Behavior, and Attitudes Review

The following review suggests some questions and issues to be addressed when evaluating motivation, behavior, and attitudes in your organization.

TABLE 8 - 2. MOTIVATION, BEHAVIOR, AND ATTITUDES REVIEW

Issues/Questions	In Place Yes	No	Partially	Action Plan (if answer is "No" or "Partially")
8.1 Are your organization's safety and health objectives stated in terms of specific behaviors and/or process improvements?				
8.2 Do training and education opportunities support the achievement of these objectives?				
8.3 Do employees receive positive reinforcement for safety and health performance/process improvement?				
8.4 Is safety and health integrated within your organization's management style and culture?				
8.5 Do communications effectively support safety and health?				
8.6 Are your safety and health communications prioritized?				

TABLE 8 - 2. MOTIVATION, BEHAVIOR, AND ATTITUDES REVIEW Continued

Issues/Questions	In Place Yes	No	Partially	Action Plan (if answer is "No" or "Partially")
8.7 Is your communication program(s) evaluated?				
8.8 Is safety and health achievement recognized at the organizational level?				
8.9 Is safety and health achievement recognized at the employee level?				
8.10 Do you obtain employee input about safety and health management processes?				

References

Books

Bauer RA. Communication as transaction. *The Obstinate Audience,* DE Payne (ed.). Ann Arbor, MI: Foundation for Research on Human Behavior, 1965.

Cohen A. Protective behaviors in the workplace. *Taking Care: Understanding and Encouraging Self-protective Behavior,* N Weinstein (ed.). Cambridge, England: Cambridge University Press, 1987.

Kanfer R. Motivation theory and industrial and organizational psychology. *Handbook of Industrial & Organizational Psychology,* MD Dunnette, LM Hough (eds.). Palo Alto, CA: Consulting Psychologists Press, 1990.

Sulzer-Azaroff B. Behavioral approaches to occupational health and safety. *Handbook of Organizational Behavior Management,* L Fredriksen (ed.). New York: John Wiley & Sons, 1982.

Weiss H. Learning theory and industrial and organizational psychology. *Handbook of Industrial & Organizational Psychology,* MD Dunnette, LM Hough (eds.). Palo Alto, CA: Consulting Psychologists Press, 1990.

Articles

Cohen A, Cleveland B. Safety program practices in record-holding plants. *Professional Safety* 28(3):26-33, 1983.

Cohen A, Smith M, Anger W. Self-protective measures against workplace hazards. *Journal of Safety Research* 11:121-131, 1979.

DeJoy D. A behavioral-diagnostic model for self-protective behavior in the workplace. *Professional Safety* 31(12):26-30, 1986.

Peters R. Strategies for encouraging self-protective employee behavior. *Journal of Safety Research* 22:53-70, 1991.

Planek TW, Fearn K. Reevaluating occupational safety priorities. *Professional Safety* 10:16-21, 1993.

Planek TW. Perception equals reality. *Public Risk* 1:14-16, 1994.

Government Publications

Conard RJ. *Employee Work Practices.* NIOSH Contact Report 81-2905. Cincinnati, OH: National Institute for Occupational Safety and Health, 1983.

U.S. General Accounting Office. *Management Practices: U.S. Companies Improve Performance Through Quality Efforts,* GAO/NSIAD-91-190. Gaithersburg, MD: U.S. GAO, May 1991.

U.S. General Accounting Office. *Organizational Culture: Techniques Companies Use to Perpetuate Change of Beliefs and Values,* GAO/NSIAD- 92-105. Gaithersburg, MD: U.S. GAO, February 1992.

Other information sources

Planek TW. The use of safety posters and other mass media in highway safety. *Aspects techniques de la securité/routiére,* Index 39-9-69. Fonds d'Etudes et de Recherches pour la Securité Routiére (ed.) Published in Brussels, Belgium, 1969.

EXECUTIVE SUMMARY — ELEMENT 9

Today, organizations must comply with a multitude of new regulations, which typically include training requirements and standards. In the United States, OSHA (Occupational Safety and Health Administration), MSHA (Mine Safety and Health Administration), DOT (Department of Transportation), FAA (Federal Aviation Administration), USCG (U.S. Coast Guard) and the EPA (Environmental Protection Agency) specify training standards in their regulations. Similarly, specific directives in the European Union's (EU) Framework Directive include training requirements. ISO 9000, which is a set of universal quality system standards, requires training in its first three phases.

While regulations have historically established minimum standards, companies that want to achieve excellence in safety and health must set their own corporate standards as well. They must determine whether a problem is attributable to training, identify characteristics of effective training, evaluate training programs, implement best training practices and manage the training process.

Once a company has defined its training standards, it can select training that will meet its needs, including instruction in safety and health management, orientation, safety and health techniques and task training.

Finally, companies need to require post-training activities, such as periodic follow-up observations, contacts and retraining, to ensure that performance change is achieved. These activities promote the transfer of learning from the class to the job, which is where companies will see a return on their training investment.

Element 9

TRAINING AND ORIENTATION

Training and education are among the most important functions in an organization today, because knowledge is growing exponentially. Information has become *the* commodity of the future; learning is how it is acquired.

The term *learning organization* was introduced by Peter Senge of the Massachusetts Institute of Technology. Central to his philosophy is his belief that "superior performance depends on superior learning." Whether a company strives to attain superior performance through a continuous improvement model, a quality program, corporate re-engineering or any other strategy, its employees must be provided with appropriate learning opportunities. Like quality and productivity, learning must be built into the total business process. It must become a systemic effort, not just an add-on.

The entire issue of learning/training/education has undergone significant changes. Some of the issues involved in the shift of how these issues are perceived (paradigm change) are highlighted in Table 9-1.

TABLE 9 - 1. TRAINING/EDUCATION ISSUES: CHANGING PERCEPTIONS

Issues	Traditional	Emerging
Job Tenure	Lifetime job; one profession	Several different jobs, employers, may switch fields/professions
Formal schooling	Once completed, seldom returned	Likely to return for courses, certificates, degree programs
Employer rationale for training	Train in the company's way of doing business; job skills	Financial-too costly not to train employees; regulatory-civil and criminal penalities; quality-increases productivity and adds value
Training topics	Limited range, specfic skills	Wide range; computer, safety, health and environment, management, regulatory, etc.
Learning resources	Few: school, employer, books	Many: traditional plus workshops, multimedia, distance learning, etc.

Training Standards

In the United States, Canada and the European Union (EU), management is being held responsible for implementing a multitude of new government regulations—most of which begin with directives for management action. Employers are responsible for meeting the training standards set by regulatory agencies that have jurisdiction in the location of operation and sometimes in the countries in which their products/services are sold.

In addition, employers are often compelled by financial factors, public perception and employee/union relations to provide effective, quality training for employees. To do this, employers must set their own standards for training, some of which may be adapted from resources made available through such professional training associations as the National Society for Performance and Instruction (NSPI) or the American Society for Training and Development (ASTD).

Regulatory training standards

Legislative directives in many countries require employers to be responsible for safe and healthful work conditions and for the control programs needed to provide them. Whether companies use engineering controls, administrative programs or personal protective equipment, training is normally needed to make the approach work. For example, ventilation controls may be of little use if employees do not know how to operate them.

Despite the intention of regulations, historically they have established only a minimum standard. Companies that wanted to achieve excellence in safety and health have set their own corporate standards.

Among important changes in recent legislative directives are increased requirements for documentation and record keeping in the United States, Canada, Europe and other areas of the world.

1. **U.S. training standards**

   In the United States, companies are responsible for knowing which federal, state and local regulations apply to their business. Many regulations specify training standards or training performance.

   While there are many regulatory agencies at the federal level, three of the most important ones for safety and health in business and industry are OSHA (Occupational Safety and Health Administration), MSHA (Mine Safety and Health Administration), and the EPA (Environmental Protection Agency).

   Many OSHA regulations have training requirements. Among those that require training are hazard communication, bloodborne pathogens, hearing conservation, powder-actuated tools, asbestos regulations, forklift tractor operations, process safety management, fire and emergency rescue, first aid/CPR, etc.

2. **European training standards**

   In Europe, the safety and health regulations of individual countries are gradually being blended through the legislation of the European Union (EU). In 1987 the EU adopted Article 118A, which focused on safety and health issues. In 1989 it adopted a Framework Directive (Directive 89/391/EEC), which established general guidelines to prevent occupational risk. Specific directives that are subordinate to the framework have been established and others are currently under development. EU legislation is performance-based.

   Recently, Great Britain implemented the 1992 Workplace Regulations, which define a "six-pack" of performance-based safety and health regulations. These incorporate specific training requirements.

3. **ISO 9000—international quality assurance**

   In 1987, the International Organization for Standardization (Geneva, Switzerland) developed ISO 9000. These standards were adopted by the EU as a means to assure customers of quality among member nations. More than 35 countries worldwide have adopted ISO 9000.

   ISO 9000 is a set of five universal quality system standards. They state requirements but do not dictate how to meet them. ISO certification is accomplished by a third-party audit. Training is required in the first three ISO phases, as shown in Table 9-2.

TABLE 9 - 2. ISO TRAINING REQUIREMENTS

Phase	Objectives	Training
1	Gain management commitment and involvement and develop a strategic plan	Senior management receives an introductory session to ISO 9000, then works to develop a plan.
2	Develop an organization to implement ISO 9000	Train the people who will be implementing the standards, so they are familiar with them.
3	Identify and develop procedures, policies, and practices to meet requirements; prepare a quality manual and documenting system	Include a training program that provides instruction and hands-on experience in writing the manual. Extensive training is required for people who will be conducting the internal ISO 9000 audits.
4	Achieve independent registration	

4. **Other country training standards**

Canada has regulatory occupational health and safety standards that are similar in intent to those in the United States. They differ in three major areas: who operates and funds the programs, whether worker involvement is mandated, and whether enforcement is more likely to be achieved through penalties (United States) or enforcement presence (Canada). These differences are under study by both governments. In fact, NAFTA has stimulated interest in exchanging information about how workers are protected in the United States, Canada and Mexico.

Company training standards and controls

Organizations provide training for their employees to improve or maintain a competitive position in the marketplace. To accomplish this, two objectives must be achieved:

1. Trainees must *acquire* useful knowledge and skills in classes (or on the job).

2. Trainees must *apply* the new knowledge and skills to their jobs and improve performance with practice and feedback.

On-the-job performance improvement translates into improved bottom-line results for an organization. Whether it has training standards or not, the company should examine information and guidelines that are used in the training and development profession. Here are six important considerations that will help a company achieve more effective results.

1. **Determine the nature of the training problem.**

   Ascertain whether or not a problem that has been diagnosed can be resolved by a training program. For example, when sales are down, companies often conclude that their sales representatives need sales training. Actually, the problem may be a combination of other factors, such as inefficient order processing or poor quality. Training solutions will *not* solve non-training-related problems.

2. **Note the paradigm shift in training.**

   Changes in learning theory and practice are causing changes in the way schools and businesses teach. Old methods—such as lecturing to students who are seated in rows—are gradually being replaced by techniques that achieve significantly better results. Driving these changes is new research on learning conducted at such universities as Johns Hopkins and Washington University. Two differences are highlighted in Table 9-3.

TABLE 9 - 3. PARADIGM SHIFT IN TRAINING

Issues	Traditional	Emerging
Theory	Subject-oriented; education theories	Performance-oriented; neuroscience, psychology, philosophy, education
Learning/ media	Passive, listening; print, film, overhead, lecture	Active, doing; multimedia, simulations, case studies, activities, coaching

3. **Apply the characteristics of effective training.**

   Effective training programs share certain characteristics. They:

   - begin with behavioral objectives
   - build on adult learning principles
   - appeal to many learning styles
   - appeal to people from diverse cultures and experiences
   - make learning memorable and experiential
   - promote teamwork
   - use instructional design principles and phased development
   - select appropriate media

4. **Evaluate your training programs.**

   As companies struggle to maintain competitiveness, training becomes an ongoing process. It thus becomes increasingly important to measure company return on investment in this activity. The third and fourth levels of evaluation provide the kind of information companies really need to assess their training.

   - *Level 1—Reactions:* How do participants rate the training? This is typically determined through anonymous questionnaires at the end of a program.

   - *Level 2—Classroom assessment:* Knowledge gained can be measured by providing pre- and post-tests based on behavioral objectives.

   - *Level 3—On-the-job assessment:* Observe participants' performance, use self-reports of skill improvements, conduct proficiency tests, etc. The goal is to measure the on-the-job skills developed by the training.

   - *Level 4—Organization improvement:* The effects of the training on the organization are usually put into financial terms, such as return on investment (ROI). Calculate results by changes in incidents, scrap, etc.

5. **Use best practices in the training area.**

   There are many guidelines available for people who are specifying, buying or developing training materials. One of the most important features of training materials is the opportunity they provide for people to do things with the information. In short, the more "performance," the better the learning, as reflected in this guideline.

People remember	Of what they
10%	read
20%	hear
30%	see
50%	hear and see
70%	say
90%	say and do

Some consideration of basic learning principles is valid whether the learning is in the class or in a work area. Training materials should be based on key principles of learning, such as reinforcement, knowledge of results, practice, meaningfulness, selective learning, frequency, recall, primacy, intensity and transfer of training (see *Accident Prevention Manual for Business & Industry: Administration & Programs,* 10th edition, 1992).

6. Manage the training process.

The training process in a company must be managed, much as any other business function is managed. The following are some of the key features of this process:

- *Training policy.* A written statement should be developed to cover the organization's policy on training. The policy should define training programs for all levels of management and employees. It should reinforce the principle that safety training is good business and can actually improve production and performance rather than interfere with it. A strong policy will help a company fulfill its safety and health missions and regulatory and legal obligations.

- *Training budgets.* Management must establish training budgets. If managers have been provided with safety and health management training as discussed below, they will have realized the many benefits of safety and health training, determined their company's current position, and established goals for improvement. Training budgets flow best out of this process.

  Safety and health training should be a component of other types of training, as well as a separate topic when appropriate. The message should be that safety and health are elements in the entire system of business operations. It is often easy to demonstrate that training costs can be recovered by preventing just one injury or occupational illness to one employee.

  Costs of training should include such items as:

  - course materials (purchase, develop in-house)

  - physical space, equipment

  - personnel staffing and/or consultants (trainers, administration)

  - employee salaries and consultant fees

  - outside training fees

  - other employee costs—transportation, meals, lodging, etc.

- *Audience/program identification.* Decisions must be made regarding the participants and the program. Examine risks to different employee groups and set priorities. Company injury and illness data can provide historical information. Examining work procedures can prevent future incidents from occurring and is a forward-looking approach in determining training needs.

  An example of an audience/program matrix is shown in Table 9-4.

TABLE 9 - 4. AUDIENCE/PROGRAM TRAINING MATRIX

Training Area	Operators	Maintenance	Emergency Coordination	Management	Supervision	Contract
Incident Investigation						
Confined Spaces						

In addition, it is usually necessary to identify training taken by specific employees. This may be cross-referenced to an employee training matrix such as the example shown in Table 9-5.

TABLE 9 - 5. EMPLOYEE TRAINING MATRIX

Safety & Health Topics

Employee	Electrical Safety	Confined Spaces	Ergonomics	Machine Safeguarding	Materials Handling	Auditing
Pat						

- *Scheduling.* Making time for training is a difficult task in most companies. Schedule training so that it does not greatly interfere with production demands and notify employees in advance. Also, allow time for follow-up practice, coaching and other activities.

- *Documentation (record keeping).* Regulatory agencies and quality assurance programs have increased their emphasis on record keeping. Ascertain what records are required for meeting regulatory standards.

  Required training data: Historically, training information, such as training programs attended, dates of training, location of training and purpose of training (initial, refresher, remedial), has been kept in standard employee records. Today, additional data may need to be kept: method of evaluation (written test, performance), evaluation scores, training methods, instructor, etc.

Other uses for data: Data has other valuable uses, such as demonstrating company commitment in a lawsuit or planning future training budgets by examining the effectiveness and costs of past training programs.

Access to data: Companies must have a written policy identifying who is allowed to access training records and under what conditions.

Types of Training

Safety management training

Safety management training is directed to senior management for the basic reason that "change begins at the top." No matter how outstanding a company is today, it must promote safety and health if it is to thrive or even survive tomorrow. Safety and health programs can have a dramatic effect on reducing costs and improving the quality of the workplace.

Safety and health programs for management should contain:

- *Information* about the types of safety and health goals that need to be set, how they can be measured and their achievement recognized and the types of programs needed to achieve them.

- *Processes* that can be used for implementation. For example:

  □ Collect and analyze company data. The data must be factual, accurate, credible, concise, comparative and in the language of finance.

  □ Create a vision for the company's performance in safety and health and integrate it with other business issues, like quality.

  □ Communicate both upstream and downstream. To communicate effectively, build credibility, present solutions to problems and follow company protocol.

Orientation training

Most companies offer orientation programs for new employees. Orientation training is one of the best introductions a company can provide for its employees. It is generally agreed that new employees are more prone to work-related incidents. This is attributed to the inexperience of new workers, their unfamiliarity with procedures and facilities and their overzealousness to do the work.

While many factors contribute to injuries, many injuries and illnesses can be prevented through new-employee safety and health orientation. Collect statistics at your facility by investigating the relationship between new employees and injuries.

Who are new employees? This category may include the following:

- New hires—any job, even office employees

- Employees who have been promoted, transferred, reassigned or relocated

- Employees returning from extended leave (e.g., medical leave)

- Employees working in a new process or with new equipment or new procedures

- Employees working in a modified process or with modified equipment or procedures

- Seasonal employees (e.g., summer help)

What topics are covered? New-employee orientation must be supported by management and supervisors. Some new-employee orientation topics focus exclusively on safety and health; others will mix safety, productivity, quality and other issues. Topics may include incident reporting and first aid/medical treatment procedures, hazard communication, personal protective equipment, fire protection prevention, natural disaster protection, emergency response and equipment use.

What are the criteria for evaluating commitment to orientation? How bona fide is a company's new orientation program? Examine these issues.

- Timing: Certain topics must be covered before beginning the job.

- Management commitment: Does management provide resources?

- Supervisor commitment: Do they actively participate?

- Goals: Are safety and health linked to quality and productivity?

- Testing: Are new employees tested to ensure understanding of the training subjects?

- Follow-up: Is follow-up done periodically to maintain the focus?

Safety technique training

Safety technique training often originates from manufacturer recommendations, from government regulations, industry "best practices" or from company/employee work practices.

1. **Manufacturer recommendations**
   Companies that manufacture equipment—whether personal protective equipment or large electrical equipment such as turbine generators—recommend that employees be taught how to use/work with their products. Instructions usually accompany the product. Training may be provided by the employer or by the manufacturer. Its purpose is to ensure the safe and proper use of the equipment, which may influence verdicts/awards in the event of an injury or illness.

2. **Government regulations**

   Some OSHA regulations require that employees be taught safe work practices. Regulations that mandate this kind of training include hazard communication, electrical safety work practices, bloodborne pathogens, emergency response planning and others.

   Some regulations, such as OSHA's Electrical Safety-Related Work Practices Regulation, 1910.331-1910.335, specify such training issues as who must be trained, where training can take place and the kind of training required for different types of workers.

3. **Company/employee work practices**

   Companies must be sure that their work practices include those recommended by manufacturers or required by government regulations. In addition, the company is likely to require additional safety technique training that is site-specific.

Task training

Task training is an outcome of the systematic examination of a task in which all loss exposures associated with the task have been identified. Task training is particularly applicable to tasks that involve physical movement that puts employees in at-risk situations.

The focus of task training has been to reduce hazards that pose threats to employees' immediate safety, but it is equally important to examine threats to employees' long-term health. Any job that requires employees to use repetitive motion and force or poor posture, or that precludes rest periods, can result in physical fatigue and injury. The result can be a long-term, chronic illness called cumulative trauma disorder (CTD). Assembly line workers who perform repetitive tasks or office workers who work for hours at a keyboard are at risk.

It is important to consider what qualifications are required of the people who will develop and/or teach task training. For example, an ergonomics expert or consultant may be required to help eliminate injuries from repetitive motion tasks. It is also important during the task identification and subsequent process to assure that any unusual physical or mental requirements essential to performing the job are made known to human resources so that they can be established as job requirements.

Post-Training Events

Companies that use learning to promote growth connect learning performance to job requirements and performance measurements (e.g., performance reviews). Furthermore, the job must reward new learning or it will not be put into practice. Supervisors, managers and peers must value and support what was learned in training, or the results will not be translated into performance changes in the workplace.

To achieve performance change, build the following post-training events into all training. This enables people to transfer the learning from the class to the job.

- *In-facility activities.* Take the principles learned in the training and apply them to the job through in-facility activities. Allow time for assignments.

- *Debriefing sessions.* After completing in-facility activities, provide debriefing sessions so participants can discuss the results of their efforts on the job and how to handle barriers/problems.

- *Job assignments.* Keep the time short between training and using skills.

- *Job observations/performance feedback.* Observe training participants on the job. Provide praise, correct mistakes and retrain.

- *Public praise, recognition.* Positive reinforcement is one of the most effective ways to get the desired behavior repeated.

Periodic observations/contacts

After training and follow-up activities have been completed, keep up the desired performance by periodically giving employees more positive reinforcement. Use job observations to provide one-on-one coaching and review opportunities; use safety meetings and job safety analysis information for the same purposes for a group or for individuals. Other techniques to achieve these results may also be used.

Safety and Health Training Review

Review your company's training policies and practices using the review that follows. Identify those items that are already in place; develop action plans for those not in place. These issues/questions are suggestions, and the list is not exhaustive. You should have many issues and questions of your own to add.

TABLE 9 - 6. SAFETY AND HEALTH TRAINING REVIEW

| Issues/Questions | In Place | | | Action Plan |
	Yes	No	Partially	(if answer is "No" or "Partially")
9.1 Do policy statements and practices support your company as a "learning organization"?				
9.2 Is the management team kept well informed of U.S. and international regulations that apply to the company and that specify training?				
9.3 Do training standards and controls ensure acquisition and application of training topics?				
9.4 Are training outcomes evaluated?				
9.5 Is the training process managed with budgets, schedules, records, value, etc.?				
9.6 Are safety and health programs provided for management?				

TABLE 9 - 6. SAFETY AND HEALTH TRAINING REVIEW Continued

Issues/Questions	In Place Yes	No	Partially	Action Plan (if answer is "No" or "Partially")
9.7 Is orientation training provided to appropriate employees with sufficient topics and measurable criteria?				
9.8 Is safety techniques training provided?				
9.9 Is task training provided where appropriate?				
9.10 Is training followed up with activities, observation, feedback, recognition, etc.?				
9.11 Are periodic observations and contacts made to keep up desired performances?				

References

Books

National Safety Council. *Accident Prevention Manual for Business & Industry: Administration & Programs,* 10th ed. Itasca, IL: NSC, 1992.

National Safety Council. *Supervisors' Safety Manual,* 8th ed. Itasca, IL: NSC, 1993.

Bird FE, Germain GL. *Practical Loss Control Leadership,* 2nd ed. Loganville, GA: International Loss Control Institute, 1992.

Broad ML, Newstrom JL. *Transfer of Training.* New York: Addison-Wesley Publishing Company, Inc., 1992.

Briggs LJ, et al. *Instructional Design: Principles and Applications,* 2nd ed. Englewood Cliffs, NJ: Educational Technology Publications, 1991.

Caine RN, Caine G. *Making Connections: Teaching and the Human Brain.* Alexandria, VA: Association for Supervision and Curriculum Development, 1991.

Gardner H. *Frames of Mind: The Theory of Multiple Intelligences.* New York: Basic Books, Inc., 1985.

Kirkpatrick D. "Evaluation" in the *Training and Development Handbook,* 3rd ed., RL Craig, ed. Sponsored by the American Society for Training and Development. New York: McGraw-Hill, 1987.

Kanter RM. *The Change Masters: Innovation and Entrepreneurship in the American Corporation.* New York: Simon & Schuster, Inc., 1983.

Kline P. *The Everyday Genius.* Arlington, VA: Great Ocean Publishers, 1988.

Mager RF. *Preparing Instructional Objectives,* 2nd ed. Belmont, CA: David S. Lake Publishers, 1984.

Margulies N. *Mapping Inner Space.* Tucson, AZ: Zephyr Press, 1991.

Rose C. *Accelerated Learning.* England: Accelerated Learning Systems Ltd., 1985.

Rummler GA, Brache AP. *Improving Performance: How to Manage the White Space on the Organization Chart.* San Francisco: Jossey-Bass, 1990.

Senge PM. *The Fifth Discipline: The Art & Practice of the Learning Organization.* New York: Doubleday/Currency, 1991.

Walton M. *Deming Management at Work.* New York: G.P. Putnam's Sons, 1990.

Articles

Ballard, J. Safety in the new Europe. *Occupational Hazards,* March 1992.

Hockman KK. Taking the mystery out of quality. *Training & Development,* July 1992.

Hughes MS. Europe's mixture of diverse customs poses challenge to EEC safety goals. *Occupational Health & Safety* (England), October 1993.

Lamparter WC. Introducing ISO 9000. *American Printer,* September 1993.

Vogel C. EC '92: Here comes a new set of rules. *Safety & Health,* March 1992.

Government Publication

U.S. General Accounting Office. *Occupational Safety and Health: Differences Between Program in the United States and Canada.* GAO/HRD-94-15FS. Washington, DC: U.S. GAO, December 1993.

EXECUTIVE SUMMARY — ELEMENT 10

Companies communicate various kinds of safety and health information. Needs can vary—from internal requirements for progress reports on safety goals and official summaries of safety meetings to informal communication between departments and formal communication from senior management to the entire organization. Management policies are key information to communicate. A safety and health policy statement is a key communication tool to show management's commitment and involvement.

Organizations may find it desirable to communicate with audiences other than their own employees. Effective working relationships can be fostered by establishing communications with fire and police departments and healthcare providers.

This chapter explores different forms of communications and how they can be applied to enhance understanding within the company and between the company and the larger community.

Different types of communications examined here are oral, written, actions and mechanical devices. Filters that hamper understanding include knowledge, biases, moods and physical and mental limitations.

The audience is critical to effective communications, but too often its needs are overlooked. Audience requirements affect the kinds, amount, format and timeliness of information.

■ ■ ■ ■ ■ ■ ■ ■ ■ ■ ■ ■ ■ ■ ■

ORGANIZATIONAL COMMUNICATIONS

Effective communication is critical to a successful safety and health program. Successful organizations have both formal and informal, open communication networks. Effective communication leads to commonly understood goals and, eventually, to a culture in which safety is a fully integrated component.

Everyone plays a role in ensuring that good communication occurs. For example, senior management conveys a corporate vision through policies and procedures. Safety and health directors and managers communicate the results of the safety and health improvement process to build energy and motivation.

This chapter describes many methods of communicating safety and health policies, goals and program results. In addition, it provides examples and guidelines for planning and implementing a good communications plan.

Defining Communication

Communication is an exchange of information. It is often illustrated as follows:

SENDER → INFORMATION → RECEIVER

Because the information in this example flows in only one direction, the sender has no way to ensure that the message was received and understood correctly. To be effective, communication must include feedback; it must be two-way. A more effective model is:

SENDER → INFORMATION → RECEIVER

FEEDBACK ←

With the feedback shown in this model, the sender can be more certain that the intended receiver actually received and understood the message.

Types of communication

People communicate through oral, written and nonverbal messages. Mechanical or other types of warning devices or markings are also a way to communicate safety information. Each type of communication is important in an effective safety and health program. Different situations call for different methods. Sometimes a combination of methods is needed. The selection of methods is often as important as the message itself.

Oral communication is a spoken exchange, either face-to-face or on the telephone. This method is best for communicating information quickly and informally. For example, a supervisor might discuss job procedures with an employee and demonstrate the proper way to perform a task. Direct oral exchange allows the supervisor to see the employee's response and the employee to ask any questions or to confirm that he or she understands the message.

Written communication is best for transmitting more complicated or technical information, because it can be referred to later. However, it is harder to make sure the recipient understands the message with written communication, so it may be necessary to follow up orally.

Policies and procedures, incident investigations, job safety analyses, work order requests and statistical summaries of injuries and illnesses are just a few examples of written communications common in safety and health.

The cliche "*actions* speak louder than words" is especially true when applied to safety and health. A policy can require employees to wear safety glasses, hearing protection or other types of personal protective equipment. But when managers walk through the plant wearing protective equipment, the nonverbal message employees receive is that management is serious about the safety and health of employees.

Electro/mechanical devices are another way to communicate. They include audible warnings (bells, buzzers, sirens, whistles), visible indicators (flashing lights and color-coded warnings), controls, interlocks and pressure-sensitive devices. Although some of these consist of "one-way" communications, some require correct feedback in order to proceed with a task.

Because feedback is so important for good communication, and communication is key to an effective safety and health program, many companies set up formal mechanisms for feedback. For example, some schedule regular question-and-answer sessions with employees. Several levels of management attend, and no topics are "off limits." Company newsletters can include a "letter to the editor" section where employees can ask questions. Electronic mail lets companies disseminate information quickly and has a feedback component; employees can pose questions on an electronic bulletin board as easily as at a meeting. Written surveys can probe attitudes and ask about factual knowledge. Simple approaches are also good; a suggestion box can serve as an effective communication device. The best feedback is displaying an open attitude and asking questions frequently.

Communication Filters

To improve communications, whether oral, written or nonverbal, managers need to consider any filters that keep the message from reaching the audience. Some common filters are knowledge, bias and mood. Physical or mental limitations can also serve as filters.

Knowledge filters may mean that the person receiving the message does not have the education or training to understand the message or that the sender is providing incorrect or inadequate information. For example, if employees have inadequate reading skills, they may not be able to understand written materials; those who are not fluent in English may not understand an oral communication. The sender may have similar problems and may also lack the insight and ability to adequately formulate the message. The person sending a message is responsible for making sure the receiver understands the message. When knowledge filters are present, the sender must take extra measures to ensure comprehension.

Biases can cause people to receive only part of a message or to tune it out entirely. They affect people's attitudes and how they process information.

Moods and emotions also affect how people send and receive information. When sending information, whether oral or written, managers need to consider their own moods and those of the receivers to be sure they are sending the message they intend. For example, a manager preoccupied with personal problems could easily forget to include an important detail in a safety procedure or overlook key data in a report to management. In certain circumstances, setting the communication aside and reading it later for aptness and clarity, or having it reviewed by another person, may improve the message. On the other hand, an employee who is obviously distracted in a meeting is likely to be hearing only part of the message. A prudent manager will talk with the employee after the meeting to discuss the information to make sure the message is getting through any filters.

Physical limitations, such as poor hearing or vision, can inhibit communication. The handicap need not be severe to have an effect. For example, an employee might not realize or want to admit he or she needs glasses and thus may miss information posted on a bulletin board or tv monitor. Or, an employee might have difficulty hearing but is embarrassed to ask a supervisor to repeat an instruction. Asking the employee to repeat an instruction helps ensure that the message reaches its target.

Mental limitations, where people have diminished mental capacity, can, depending upon degree, require more direct, "hands-on" communication and subsequent reinforcement.

The Audience

Because the interim objective of communication is to gain understanding, with the ultimate goal being to influence behavior, one of the first considerations is the audience's needs. What is the audience's previous knowledge as well as any physical challenges that might interfere with the message? What is their level of interest, education and experience? Do they have responsibility for the information being communicated? Just what does the audience need to know?

In safety and health, it is also important that companies identify the different audiences a program must address. Audiences and their communication needs often vary from one location to another. For example, office employees may not be familiar with jargon or terms that are common in the plant. Communicating with one audience may have different challenges from communicating with the other.

The kinds, amount, format and timeliness of information needed may also vary from one audience to another. For example, senior management needs information that is not needed by a warehouse employee.

One of the most common errors in business communications is overloading readers or listeners with more information than they need to know. For example, you may know that three different versions of a machine safeguard were used before the guard in current use. If you try to explain all of these safeguards in a safety training manual for new employees, you'll be providing information of questionable value that will only confuse them. Stick to the information the audience *needs* to know and save the rest. Try to put yourself in the place of the person receiving your communication: What information does the receiver need? Tailor your message to this need.

Regulations, Safety Procedures, Goals and Results

Among the most common kinds of safety information communicated are safety procedures, goals and results of programs to achieve the goals or to implement the procedures. Safety directors and managers with safety responsibilities use a wide variety of communication techniques depending on the situation and audience's needs. Table 10-1 defines typical situations and describes techniques to use.

TABLE 10-1: WAYS TO COMMUNICATE SAFETY INFORMATION

Communication Needs	Ways to Communicate
The organization needs frequent, informal communication with employees to update them on progress toward safety goals or to ask them to take action. It's important to be brief. Company policy may require a written summary of information.	A *memo* is a good option. For example, a manager might send a weekly memo to people in his or her department to update them on the progress toward a safety goal.
Senior management and key staffers in other areas of the company need to be informed about the status of various safety and health programs or told about progress toward previously published goals.	A *formal report* presents comprehensive and specific information in detail. A typical report includes benefits (such as reductions in workers'- compensation costs) of safety and health programs, costs and relevant statistics.
A group needs an official summary of safety meetings detailing what actions the group takes and whether they are effective or need adjusting.	*Meeting minutes* provide an ongoing history of events and are an important part of a safety and health program.
Formal communication is needed with groups or individuals outside the organization.	*Letters* that detail relevant information about a safety and health program are often sent to other companies or community groups.
Employees need information about safety and health.	An *informal talk* is a good way to present such information as safety tips, demonstrations (how to use personal protective equipment) or results of special safety programs. The talk can be supplemented with literature, such as employee booklets.
The results of safety and health programs must be presented to large groups of employees and to management.	A *formal presentation* is needed. When making a formal presentation, be sure to plan carefully and to use visual aids such as slides or overhead transparencies to summarize key information. A printed handout enhances retention of information.
Employees need ongoing reminders of key safety tips and general safety awareness.	*Posters* can provide general safety awareness and remind employees of key safety tips. While they are a valuable addition to a safety and health communication program, posters should never be used as the only method to transmit information.

TABLE 10 - 1. WAYS TO COMMUNICATE SAFETY INFORMATION Continued

Communication Needs	Ways to Communicate
A group, a manager or a whole department needs to illustrate the results of a safety program or progress toward goals for other employees.	*Charts and graphs* are especially helpful in these situations. Consider posting information (especially in chart/graph form) in a cafeteria, break room and work areas.
Employees need more information than can be presented verbally in a meeting; the information presented at meetings should be reinforced; or an employee is not able to attend the meeting.	*Handouts* such as safety and health booklets are important links in any program. Employees can read them at their own pace. Multilingual versions can help fill the gaps for employees whose first language is not English.
Management needs to provide ongoing reinforcement of training and communication of routine safety information.	*Newsletters* can be a good solution. They can include safety tips, laws and regulations, results of safety efforts (such as the number of days since a lost-time injury) and messages from management.
Managers must communicate information required by law.	In general, the format and requirements for communicating this information is prescribed by the appropriate laws and regulations.
Companies may make public statements regarding safety information.	*Material Safety Data Sheets* can be used, as can materials for "hazmat" employees (those responsible for safe handling, transportation or emergency response to incidents involving hazardous materials). A frequent strategy is to include safety information in other public communications, such as annual and quarterly reports, press releases, etc.

Public Relations and Media Management

Public relations is important for all aspects of corporate life in the 1990s, and safety and health are no exception. An effective communication program will keep in touch with groups in an organization's community as well as the local news media. Should a crisis occur that requires a company to notify the community in which the company is located, it will be handled through the established local emergency committee channels and will pertain only to incidents that can affect the surrounding community.

Working with local fire and police departments is essential to a successful emergency response program. In many cases, emergency response and community right-to-know legislation require that companies work with their local fire departments.

Keep in touch with local media: Just as showing your concern for employees and their safety and health needs often improves safe behavior on the job, showing that your organization is a concerned member of the community can improve off-the-job safety behavior by employees, their families and neighbors. The table below lists the elements of a safety and health public relations program.

TABLE 10 - 2. SAFETY AND HEALTH COMMUNICATION PROGRAM ELEMENTS

Element	Considerations
1. Relationship with fire and police departments	These agencies can help you with key aspects of your safety and health plans, such as fire safety, emergency planning and community awareness. The association may be required by legislation.
2. Relationship with medical providers	They can serve as a resource for your own programs. Also, the people in these organizations are often community leaders.
3. Written communications such as annual and quarterly reports, press releases and other public statements	These are good tools for publicizing your company's accomplishments.

An effective safety and health program will include these elements as a minimum public relations strategy. It's important to stay in touch with the community and to publicize your internal efforts to the outside community when appropriate. News releases are a good way to stay in touch with the media and other groups.

Senior Management Policies

Communication begins at the top of an organization. A company's policy statement reflects its philosophy toward safety and health. In its safety and health policy, senior management sends a message of commitment and involvement to its employees, customers and the larger community.

A sample safety and health or policy statement is shown in Figure 10-1.

FIGURE 10 - 1. SAMPLE POLICY STATEMENT

ABC Company Safety and Health Policy

Our safety and health policy is to provide safe, clean and healthful facilities for our employees. We will act in a way that ensures:

- We comply with all safety and health laws—and, in many instances, utilize a best practice approach to safety and health.

- Our business decisions incorporate our commitment to protect the safety and health of our employees and the members of communities in which we are located.

- We provide products that people can use safely.

- Our operations are reviewed regularly to see that we maintain the highest standards of safety and health in all areas.

- We encourage the health and safety of our employees through training, communication, an extensive Employee Assistance Program and a clean, safe workplace.

- Our employees are empowered to take appropriate actions on their own initiative when they encounter any threats to the safety and health of other employees, customers or members of the communities in which we operate.

Organizational Communications Review

Companies can review their existing safety and health communications programs using the questions in Table 10-3 as guidelines. Identify items that are already in place; then, develop action plans for those not in place. These are suggested issues/questions, and the list is by no means exhaustive. No doubt you will have many issues/questions of your own to add.

TABLE 10 - 3. ORGANIZATIONAL COMMUNICATIONS REVIEW

| Issues/Questions | In Place | | | Action Plan |
	Yes	No	Partially	(if answer is "No" or "Partially")
10.1 Is there a safety and health policy statement?				
10.2 Are written procedures in place supporting the safety and health policy?				
10.3 Does management routinely communicate on safety and health subjects?				
10.4 Do informal communications with employees occur to present safety tips, update them on progress toward safety goals, or ask them to take action?				

TABLE 10 - 3. ORGANIZATIONAL COMMUNICATIONS REVIEW Continued

Issues/Questions	In Place Yes	No	Partially	Action Plan (if answer is "No" or "Partially")
10.5 Are minutes prepared from each safety meeting?				
10.6 Are the results of safety and health programs presented to employees and management?				
10.7 Are safety visuals, such as posters, used to promote general safety awareness and remind employees of key safety issues?				
10.8 Are safety and health publications, such as booklets, provided for employees so they can read them at their own pace? Are multilingual versions available?				

TABLE 10 - 3. ORGANIZATIONAL COMMUNICATIONS REVIEW Continued

| Issues/Questions | In Place | | | Action Plan |
	Yes	No	Partially	(if answer is "No" or "Partially")
10.9 Does management communicate information required by law through training and education, such as that contained in Material Safety Data Sheets or materials for "hazmat" or "hazcom" employees?				

References

Books

Bird FE, Germain GL. *Practical Loss Control Leadership,* 2nd ed. Loganville, GA: International Loss Control Institute, 1992.

National Safety Council. *Accident Prevention Manual for Business & Industry: Administration & Programs,* 10th ed. Itasca, IL: NSC, 1992.

National Safety Council. *Supervisors' Safety Manual,* 8th ed. Itasca, IL: NSC, 1993.

Articles

Gavin D. Building a learning organization. *Harvard Business Review,* 71:4:78- 91, 1993.

Ishoy K, Swan P. Creating a mission statement. *Performance & Instruction,* 31:10:11-15, 1992.

Johnson P. How I turned a critical public into useful consultants. *Harvard Business Review,* 71:1:56-66, 1993.

Lee D. The vision thing. *Training,* 30:2:25-3, 1993.

White D. How to manage a multilingual work force. *Safety and Health,* January 1994.

Packaged Training Program

National Safety Council. Agenda 2000® Safety Health Environment Program. Itasca, IL: NSC, 1992.

EXECUTIVE SUMMARY — ELEMENT 11

Effective management and control of external exposures are an integral part of a company's successful safety and health program and key to its overall plan for risk management. Senior management needs to consider issues related to five major kinds of external exposure that can put the company at risk for potential liability.

Contractors, vendors, products produced by the company, public liability and natural disasters can expose the company to incidents, injuries and illnesses, as well as to substantial financial loss. Management should establish policies for addressing each exposure.

Companies can take proactive steps to assess and prioritize risks. Techniques for dealing with them include prequalifying contractors and vendors; monitoring changes in standards and regulations (especially in the global marketplace) and the impact of those changes; and adopting a proactive approach to minimizing exposure.

11

MANAGEMENT AND CONTROL OF EXTERNAL EXPOSURES

Effective management and control of external exposures are essential for a successful safety and health program. Without an awareness of potential liability from external exposures, coupled with a comprehensive plan to identify and minimize exposure in those areas in which problems can arise, a company is at risk—not only for incidents, injuries and illnesses but also for substantial financial loss.

If external exposures are not well managed and controlled, they can cost a company time and money. They can result in loss of business and reputation. And, they can have political repercussions at the local, state and even federal level.

External exposures include any influence on risk that arises outside the boundaries of company property or is caused by a third party. Common types of external exposures are (but are not limited to) those that result from actions connected with:

- on-site contractors
- vendors
- products produced by the company
- public liability
- natural disasters

Effective programs for managing and controlling external exposures need to incorporate these key characteristics:

- Senior management is strongly committed to—and involved in—the company's comprehensive safety and health program. Management and control of external exposures are integral to the organization's overall plan for risk management.

- Underlying administrative or procedural systems are in place and operational. Senior management is not involved in the details of these systems but is assured that the systems are there and are working. At a minimum, such programs include the following components:

  - Assessing external exposure to risk

  - Being aware of liabilities, legislation, regulations and required licensing

  - Monitoring changes in legislation, regulations and licensing; tracking of phase-in and compliance dates and modifying of safety programs accordingly

  - Measuring performance by objective indexes, such as OSHA recordables

  - Timely reporting of significant matters so they can be closely monitored by management

Contractor Control Programs

Businesses that bring outside workers on-site or contract for the services of workers employed by an outside firm need effective contractor control programs. This reduces their exposure to potential losses. Such programs must be carefully developed and managed.

Host employers need to establish guidelines that afford the contractor's workers at least the same quality of safety and health protection as the employer's own work force receives.

Depending upon the terms of the contract, employers and contractors are often responsible for the safety of their own personnel. However, despite contract language, host employers may not be able to avoid liability if incidents or injuries occur. Many states hold that the host employer is in charge—implying that the host employer bears the ultimate responsibility for safety. An effective contractor control program provides oversight functions with respect to contractors.

Preplanning is one of the program's most important elements. As part of preplanning, the host employer should designate a coordinator to be responsible for contracted activities (including construction). A company needs to protect its interest by assigning safety and health responsibilities to a trained, experienced individual.

Assuring contractor safety

As a first step in preplanning specific projects, the host employer must assess hazards and exposures. Is fatality a real possibility if safety procedures are not followed? Does the project for which the contractor is being hired require special training—for example, in confined spaces? Or, is the potential for hazard and exposure less because of the nature of the project? For instance, does the project require welding around exposed gas lines or merely painting a fence?

The degree of risk—the probability of loss and its potential magnitude— determines how rigorously the host employer needs to screen contractors.

In addition, the host employer needs to establish minimum guidelines for safety and health issues, making sure that all regulatory requirements—such as obtaining necessary permits—have been addressed by contractors.

To minimize risk, use specific safety performance criteria for selecting contractors. Companies that contract for outside services need to make sure the contractors they use have written safety and health programs and good safety records. Many companies prequalify contractors, requiring them to submit information on their past safety performance. This data is reviewed, and only companies with acceptable safety records are invited to submit proposals. Before the bidding process begins, contractors should provide the following information for the preceding three years:

- OSHA total recordable injury and illness incidence rate

- OSHA days away from work case incidence rate

- Experience modification ratios (EMR) (workers' compensation loss versus premium history)

Check contractors' experience modification ratio against that of your own company. To reduce your risk as the host employer, consider limiting contractors under consideration to those who have an EMR equal to or less than yours. If a contractor's EMR is worse than yours, explore what has been done in the past 18 months to improve the program. The contractor may have implemented a safety program but the EMR has yet to be affected.

As part of the prequalification process, ask contractors to submit documents that indicate their commitment to safety. These documents can be specified in the request for proposal (RFP). For instance, a host employer may request a contractor's written safety program. Additionally, the host employer may ask for a copy of the contractor's safety orientation program, workers' compensation management program and the contractor's enforcement and disciplinary procedures for safety violations.

Contractors may be asked how they would budget for safety equipment for the project or to describe their program for compliance with applicable regulatory requirements. For example, will personal protective equipment be required? If so, what will be supplied? Are training and maintenance procedures for contractor-supplied equipment adequate? Are they performed on schedule?

The host employer will want to know what criteria the proposed contractor uses to hire subcontractors. Everything the host employer requires of the general contractor must be extended to the subcontractors—for example, screening workers for drug and substance abuse.

Contract language should clearly spell out that the contractor agrees to comply with all federal, state and local safety regulations and with applicable consensus standards, such as ANSI A10.33, "Safety and Health Program Requirements for Multi-Employer Projects."

For maximum efficiency, the contractor should designate specific persons to respond to the host employer's safety and health needs. These persons should spearhead all of the contractor's safety-required activities, including:

- prescreening workers and new hires for drug and substance abuse
- verifying required training and/or certification
- selecting and providing safety and health equipment and supplies
- providing a safety and health orientation for the contract workers

If the contracted work is complex or performed over an extended period of time, the host employer's staff coordinator should monitor the contractor's safety performance periodically. The coordinator can perform safety inspections, review accident reports and have the contractor provide OSHA logs on a regular basis.

Verifying contractor insurance and appropriate training

Verification of contractor insurance is an essential part of an effective contractor control program. A request for proposal should include the requirement that the contractor provide appropriate certificates of insurance and amounts, to remain in force throughout the project. Before awarding the contract for a project, the host employer needs to review the potential for loss and establish minimum limits for insurance.

The host employer's coordinator verifies the coverage, noting and tracking any expiration dates. If the project takes longer than anticipated, the insurance must be checked to be sure it is still adequate and in force.

When appropriate, especially for long-term projects, the contract administrator of the host employer may require a contractor to state as part of the certificate of insurance that the owner is an additional named insured. In addition, the coordinator may want to check the qualifications of those who train the contractor's workers. In fact, the coordinator may even attend a training session to monitor its quality and appropriateness.

Training by the contractor for the contractor's workers also must be verified. The host employer should develop procedures to ensure that:

- training needs have been identified

- personnel who conduct training have the required qualifications

- regulatory requirements have been met

- records are adequately and accurately documented

In addition to safety and health training appropriate to the project, the contractor's workers should be trained in any special characteristics or hazards the site presents. For instance, if they are working in areas with excessive noise exposure, have contractor employees been provided with hearing protection by the contractor, and do they know how to use it properly? Do they know how to store and dispose of supplies and waste?

If the contractor's employees will be working near or with hazardous chemicals, do they know what those hazards are, how to protect themselves against them and what to do in case of a chemical accident or spill? Do they share information about chemicals they bring into the host's property? It is up to the host company to coordinate hazardous materials information among all contractors working on that site who might possibly be exposed. The host company also must train contractors on what the emergency plan calls for, what signals are given in an emergency and what the contractor's employees need to do to respond to that emergency.

For example, if a contractor's employees are given respirators to carry with them at all times, do those employees have the necessary training on how to use the respirators and how to evacuate the site? Does the contractor have a written respiratory protection program and a means to address all that it requires (fitting, maintenance, medical assessment, cleaning, etc.)? Audits are a tool to help verify that appropriate, timely training has taken place.

Vendors

In order to limit hazards introduced from the outside, companies need a proactive safety and health program in place to qualify purchases of various tools, equipment, materials and supplies and to monitor purchases from vendors for compliance.

Assessing liability exposure

As a first step in identifying risk exposure, companies need to regularly review the loss-producing potential of purchased products and services. In short, what can go wrong if these products fail or do not protect employees adequately? What are the financial implications if they fail? Hazards can be ranked by probability of occurrence and rated by potential consequence.

Companies should pay special attention to PPE purchases, such as eye protection and respirators. Other key elements to be assessed include ropes and chains for moving suspended loads and equipment to move and store materials. If chemicals create a hazard and cannot be replaced by non- or less-hazardous substances, then both the hazard and the exposure to the hazard must be controlled. Purchase specifications for substances used for cleaning or maintenance need to be reviewed to be sure the cleaners don't cause or aggravate fire and health hazards. If they do, and such cleaners are the only products available to do the job, then employees and others must be appropriately protected.

Addressing exposure and ensuring protection

As a minimum, all purchasing agreements should clearly spell out the buyers' requirements. These requirements should reflect the equipment's intended use as well as any special conditions of the location where it will be used.

If the company operates in a global market, plans to do so, or buys from vendors outside the United States, its purchasing procedures also should take into account applicable international standards and directives as they are developed.

For example, the European Union's (EU) Safety of Machinery Directive (89/392/EEC) has provisions for a noise declaration. A manufacturer of machinery must furnish the user with adequate information about the noise and vibration properties of the machinery. EU directives on permissible noise emissions for construction site equipment, earth-moving machines and lawn mowers also require noise labeling.

Other EU standards being developed refer to safety-related devices—for example, two-hand controls, interlocking devices, pressure-sensitive devices and guards. Standards that parallel the United States' OSHA Lockout/Tagout standard are in various stages of development. They include "Isolation and Energy Dissipation: Prevention of Unintended/Unexpected Start-Up," which covers all forms of energy and is under the Machinery Directive 89/392/EEC; and the International Electrotechnical Commission (IEC) standard IEC 204-1/1992, for which amendments are being prepared.

As companies specify purchases of materials, supplies, and equipment, they may also want to consider the ISO 9000 Standard Series. These generic standards address aspects of quality assurance.

The process, organizational structure, procedures and resources that manufacturers and suppliers use to control variables in the production of products is called a system. ISO 9000 standards are being adopted globally for quality systems.

The ISO 9000 Standard Series was intended to be advisory in nature; however, conformance to those standards is being required in purchasing specifications with increasing frequency. In some cases, compliance with one of the ISO 9000 standards (or their equivalent) has been or will be mandated by a United States, foreign national or regional government body.

For maximum effectiveness in controlling external exposure from vendors, management needs cross-functional teamwork among safety and health professionals, plant operations personnel, engineers and purchasing agents. Questions to be addressed include the following:

- Is there a procedure that reviews the safety of materials, tools and equipment before they are bid on and purchased? Is the procedure periodically updated and evaluated for effectiveness?

- Are the plant's processes periodically reviewed, especially as markets and technology develop and change? Are ergonomic aspects considered when tools and equipment are selected?

- Can production processes be modified to minimize waste or reduce hazards of waste disposal? If so, have purchasing specifications been reviewed and, if necessary, changed to reflect those modifications?

- Does the company track and monitor phase-in dates or changes in regulatory requirements, and are specifications for incoming products changed accordingly?

In the United States, to comply with OSHA and EPA regulations on emissions of volatile organic substances, many companies that previously used them are switching to aqueous cleaning solutions.

Environmental concerns that affect the selection of products and vendors reach beyond national boundaries. In fall 1992, representatives from more than 85 countries met to amend the "Montreal Protocol on Substances That Deplete the Ozone Layer," an international treaty. The amendments move the phaseout deadlines for chlorofluorocarbons (CFCs) and certain other chemicals to Jan. 1, 1996. However, most existing refrigeration and air-conditioning equipment (including building air conditioners) relies on CFCs. Because CFCs for servicing will be unavailable, companies need to begin planning alternative purchases.

If used machinery or equipment is purchased, has it been checked for safety? Does it comply with current OSHA and consensus standards? If end-user hardware for guarding is to be installed, is the type of guarding appropriate for how the machine will be used? Have guards been installed correctly?

Have safe shipping methods been specified? Are all hazardous materials labeled with Department of Transportation (DOT)-specified shipping labels? Do Material Safety Data Sheets (MSDS) accompany all incoming chemicals or products that contain hazardous chemicals? Vendors must be required, if appropriate, to label incoming products with information that meets the requirements of the Hazard Communication standard.

Companies can minimize their risk of exposure from vendors by controlling the quality of materials and services they purchase. To that end, management should consider these steps:

- Establish a policy that any deviations from material specifications requires the written permission of the engineering or design departments. Any deviations should be reviewed by a safety and health professional.

- Compile a list of "approved" suppliers and products.

- Furnish suppliers with detailed requirements to avoid misunderstanding or misinterpretation.

- Develop procedures to monitor suppliers.

Product Safety Control

Product safety issues represent a significant financial risk for companies. Product liability affects not only industrial capital goods firms, but also manufacturers of consumer durables (such as autos and appliances) and industrial equipment and machinery companies. In addition, product safety concerns are issues for wholesalers, distributors, retailers, service and repair organizations and various contracting firms.

Adverse effects of product liability exposure can include:

- plant closings

- discontinuance of existing products

- increased insurance costs

- employee layoffs

- loss of market share

- termination of research on product lines judged liability-prone

- decisions not to introduce newly developed products

As a first step in minimizing exposure, management needs to understand all possible bases for claims and develop a comprehensive program to address product safety issues.

A product is more than just the item sold. A product includes the sales literature, labels, manuals and advertising supplied with the item, attached to it, printed on it, or printed or sent separately after purchase. A product also includes the parts, accessories and special tools supplied by the manufacturer to the customer.

Once a product has been sold, it is a potential source of legal liability for the manufacturer or anyone else in the distribution chain if it is involved in an incident, injury or illness. Undesirable product incident exposure can also occur with products in use but no longer being manufactured.

Assessing exposure

Many areas of business activity have the potential for causing an incident that would put the company at risk. For instance, activities related to product concept, research, design, development and testing are possible sources of product liability claims. So are manufacturing and product quality assurance.

Claims can arise from a company's noncompliance with industry standards, regulations, codes and record retention practices. Warnings, instructions and information should be checked. Advertising and representations, marketing and sales, and maintenance, service and repairs are additional risk exposures. So are packaging, shipping, storage and handling.

Because all these areas can be a potential source of loss for an organization, an effective program to identify risk exposure gathers and analyzes data from all operating components. Such data can include:

- product safety hazard analysis

- loss trends

- warranty or guarantee claims

- product incidents and claim history

- production and sales volume, distribution data and use data as needed to accurately define the extent of possible future liability

Ensuring protection

Senior management can demonstrate commitment to a product safety program in several ways. A policy statement will make it clear that safety and the control of product liability losses are important company objectives. Such a policy statement should be communicated to all levels of management and all affected employees.

In addition, management needs to provide the leadership and resources necessary to implement the product safety program.

Many companies have chosen to set up product safety departments or to name a product safety coordinator. Legal and insurance specialists—either within the company or the retained attorney and insurance carrier—can be called on for help in developing a comprehensive product safety program.

Since no two companies operate the same way, there is no "best" way to organize such a program. However, a strong product safety program will include the following:

- Established guidelines and criteria to identify and evaluate product hazards and their associated potential for loss

- Basic procedures for design, development and testing of effective instructions and warning labels for product hazards that can't be eliminated

- Established guidelines and review of all printed material to be sure it is clear and conforms to laws and regulations of all federal, state and local acts, codes and directives

- Notification of any federal, state or local regulatory agency if a product is defective or doesn't comply with safety standards, codes or regulations

- Development of written procedures for recalling products, notifying the public and correcting the problem

Public Liability Exposures

A company's plan to manage and control external exposures must include consideration of its public liability. If there is a reasonable expectation that the public will be exposed to a hazard created by or arising out of company activities, a company needs to foresee those risks and take appropriate action to minimize its public liability exposure. Failure to do so can result in substantial financial loss.

Potential exposure

Fences, barricades and warning signs should control public access to hazardous areas such as construction sites. If company parking lots or sidewalks have holes, these should be fixed promptly. Excavations should be barricaded and fenced for the duration of construction work. Lighting must be adequate to identify hazards. Warning signs need to be posted.

Good housekeeping and order are "musts" for areas to which the public has access. For instance, in restaurants and stores, spills need to be cleaned promptly from floors and aisles need to be kept clear of obstructions.

Other public liability exposures are less apparent, yet management needs to be aware of responsibility for them. For example, are company premises up to date in meeting life safety codes and standards set by such organizations as the National Fire Protection Association (NFPA)?

Do waiting rooms, reception areas, cafeterias, restrooms, drinking fountains and elevators that are used by the public comply with access requirements mandated by the Americans with Disabilities Act (ADA), or with consensus standards like American National Standards Institute, ANSI/CABO A117.1-1992 "Accessible and Usable Buildings and Facilities"? Can people with mobility disabilities enter and leave the building easily? Are exit signs clearly marked?

If companies invite private individuals onto their premises, management needs to be sure procedures are in place to keep visitors out of areas in which heavy equipment (such as forklift trucks) is operating. Machines should be guarded; ramps, stairways and balconies also must be guarded properly.

Plant tours are another potential source of public liability. If visitors are touring the facility, are they provided with hard hats, safety glasses, hearing protection or safety footwear required to protect them against any hazards in the areas they may pass through? Have visitors been properly instructed in its use?

Assessing liability potential

A proactive approach to minimizing losses includes the assessment of potential liability. Management needs to know how serious a loss might be, so it can rank exposures and act accordingly. In short, management needs to ask:

- What can go wrong?

- What are the probabilities that something will go wrong?

- What would be the consequences if something does go wrong?

For instance, if the public would be at risk from unintentionally spilled or released toxic materials, management will want to give this risk a high priority. Management needs to ensure that strategies have been devised to minimize the chances of this occurring and that effective plans are in place to deal with the emergency if an incident occurs.

Disaster Preparedness

Unexpected or disastrous events can strike any organization. Natural disasters can produce major financial consequences to a company. Prudent loss control measures to mitigate against damages start with identifying and evaluating hazards: floods, hurricanes, tornadoes, earthquakes and other weather-related emergencies.

Although planning for disasters is often assigned to the safety and health professionals within an organization, senior management bears the ultimate responsibility for emergency planning. Executives need to work closely with these professionals to be sure that contingency plans have been developed to respond to these potential emergency events.

Disaster planning should be carried out with the worst-case scenario in mind. Three levels of concern are necessary:

1. Public and employee safety, both for short-term and long-term needs

2. Protection of property, operations and the environment

3. Restoring business operations to normal

Assessing potential exposure

Organizations need to assess and prioritize potential for harm to people, the environment and property during natural disasters. Senior management then should review the assessment to be sure it covers not only normal working conditions but also "what if" scenarios. For example, what is the potential for loss exposure if a disaster happens on weekends or holidays when only a skeleton staff is on hand to respond?

Regulatory considerations—including environmental—also must be taken into account in emergency response planning. If there is a possibility of environmental damage to nearby communities, operations need to meet emergency requirements of regulatory agencies.

Under Title III of the Superfund Amendments and Reauthorization Act, commonly known as SARA, government, industry and the community need to work together to develop comprehensive emergency action plans. Companies should provide detailed information about their hazardous materials to local emergency planning committees to use in developing emergency response plans for the comunities. The committees are also responsible for making the information available to the public.

In addition, Title III requires companies that have and use toxic chemicals to report any emissions of these materials into the air, land and water. If a hazardous chemical is released, companies must notify local, state and federal officials immediately, as well as the local emergency planning committee. Written reports about the incident need to be available to the community.

Senior management should have a trained and experienced person review and monitor applicable regulations and standards. Within the United States, such standards include:

- Comprehensive Environmental Response Compensation and Liability Act (CERCLA)

- Superfund Amendments and Reauthorization Act (SARA)

- OSHA's Hazardous Waste Operations and Emergency Response (29 CFR 1910.120)

- OSHA's Hazardous Communication Standard (29 CFR 1910.1200)

- Clean Air Act

- Clean Water Act

- Resource Conservation and Recovery Act (RCRA)

- Toxic Substances Control Act (TSCA)

- Federal Insecticide, Fungicide and Rodenticide Act (FIFRA)

- Comprehensive Environmental Response Compensation and Liability Act (CERCLA)

- Hazardous Materials Transportation Uniform Safety Act

- Pollution Prevention Act of 1990

Management and Control of External Exposures Review

Companies must be sure that all of their facilities comply fully with all requirements—not only to address the health and safety of employees and the community, but also to minimize public liability exposure in case of a disaster.

In general, a comprehensive emergency plan states who does what, when and where—before, during and after a disaster. Often the plan incorporates procedures that state how something is to be done.

The development of a comprehensive emergency response plan and its continuous updating is not an inexpensive undertaking. However, to fulfill its responsibilities and obligations, senior management must provide necessary financial and human resources to develop an appropriate plan, monitor implementation of its provisions and modify it as needed. The following review suggests some questions and issues to address when evaluating existing management and control of external exposures.

TABLE 11-1. MANAGEMENT AND CONTROL OF EXTERNAL EXPOSURES REVIEW

| Issues/Questions | In Place | | | Action Plan |
	Yes	No	Partially	(if answer is "no" or Partially")
11.1 Has the host employer set adequate guidelines for managing and controlling contractor programs? Have these guidelines been reviewed by the employer's legal counsel and insurance representative?				
11.2 Has the company assessed and prioritized exposure risks by project and degree of risk? Are contractors prequalified?				

TABLE 11-1. MANAGEMENT AND CONTROL OF EXTERNAL EXPOSURES REVIEW Continued

Issues/Questions	In Place Yes	No	Partially	Action Plan (if answer is "no" or Partially")
11.3 Have contractors' insurance premium limits and conditions been predetermined for each project? Are insurance coverages verified independently and tracked for expiration dates?				
11.4 Are procedures in place to monitor and update purchasing specifications to reflect changes and modifications in regulations, standards, and international directives?				
11.5 Does the company furnish suppliers with detailed requirements to avoid misunderstanding or misinterpretation?				

TABLE 11-1. MANAGEMENT AND CONTROL OF EXTERNAL EXPOSURES REVIEW Continued

| Issues/Questions | In Place | | | Action Plan |
	Yes	No	Partially	(if answer is "no" or Partially")
11.6 Has the company developed and implemented a comprehensive product safety program? Have legal counsel and insurance carriers participated in designing, developing, monitoring and updating the program?				
11.7 Are good housekeeping and order "musts" for all areas to which the public has access? Are appropriate maintenance and inspection procedures developed, followed and monitored?				
11.8 Is risk exposure periodically reviewed with legal counsel and insurance carriers? Are appropriate insurance coverages in force and monitored for expiration dates?				

TABLE 11-1. MANAGEMENT AND CONTROL OF EXTERNAL EXPOSURES REVIEW Continued

Issues/Questions	In Place Yes	No	Partially	Action Plan (if answer is "no" or Partially")
11.9 Has senior management reviewed disaster risk assessment—not only for normal conditions, but also for "what if" scenarios and "worst case" disasters?				
11.10 Has senior management named and appropriately trained a senior official and a backup person to deal with disasters? Does each have authority to make immediate or timely decisions in the event of a disaster? Are funds and personnel available on a timely basis to implement those decisions?				
11.11 Have primary and contingency plans that comply with all applicable regulations been developed to protect persons, property, operations, and the environment? to restore business operations? Have the plans been clearly communicated to management, employees, and appropriate community and government agencies?				

TABLE 11-1. MANAGEMENT AND CONTROL OF EXTERNAL EXPOSURES REVIEW Continued

| Issues/Questions | In Place | | | Action Plan |
	Yes	No	Partially	(if answer is "no" or Partially")
11.12 Have funds and staff been committed for training and refresher training as needed? Is record keeping adequate to document required training?				
11.13 Are plans periodically monitored, reviewed and updated as appropriate? Is required information on file with appropriate agencies?				

References

Books

Bird Jr., FE, Germain GL. *Practical Loss Control Leadership*, 2nd ed. Loganville, GA: International Loss Control Institute, 1990.

National Fire Protection Association. *Hazardous Materials Response Handbook*, Henry M, ed. Quincy, MA: NFPA, 1989.

Ladou J. *Occupational Health and Safety*, 2nd ed. Itasca, IL: National Safety Council, 1994.

National Safety Council. *Accident Prevention Manual for Business & Industry: Administration & Programs*, 10th ed. Itasca, IL: NSC, 1992.

National Safety Council. *Accident Prevention Manual for Business & Industry: Engineering & Technology*, 10th ed. Itasca, IL: NSC, 1992.

National Safety Council. *Guide to Americans with Disabilities Act*. Itasca, IL: NSC, 1992.

National Safety Council. *Product Safety: Management Guidelines*. Itasca, IL: NSC, 1989.

Articles

Appleby P. Healthy workplaces. *Health & Safety at Work* 15(7):14-17, 1993.

Trilateral cooperation moves forward. *ANSI Reporter* 4:1-2, 1993.

Bone J. Unlock the mystery of lockout/tagout. *Safety & Health* 4:66- 69, 1994.

Henkoff R. The hot new seal of quality. *Fortune* 127(13):116-120, 1993.

Hockman KK, Erdman DA. Gearing up for ISO 9000 registration. *Chemical Engineering* 4:128-134, 1993.

Honkasalo A, Kyttala I, Nykanen H. International noise declaration system for machinery and equipment. *Noise Control Engineering Journal* 40(1):143-150, 1993.

National Safety Council. *Global SH&E* 7/8:2, 1993.

Government Publication

U.S. Department of Labor. *Principal Emergency Response and Preparedness Requirements in OSHA Standards and Guidance for Safety and Health Programs,* OSHA Pub. No. 3122, Washington, DC: U.S. GPO 1990.

Packaged Training Program

National Safety Council. Agenda 2000® Safety Health Environment Program. Itasca, IL: NSC, 1992.

Reports

Breitenberg M. *Questions and Answers on Quality, the ISO 9000 Standard Series, Quality System Registration, and Related Issues.* NISTIR 4721. Washington DC: U.S. Department of Commerce, Technology Administration, National Institute of Standards and Technology, 1993.

Breitenberg M. *More Questions and Answers on the ISO 9000 Standard Series and Related Issues.* NISTIR 5122. Washington DC: U.S. Department of Commerce, Technology Administration, National Institute of Standards and Technology, 1993.

The Impact of Product Liability, Report 908. New York: The Conference Board, 1988.

Standards

American National Standards Institute. ANSI A10.33-1992, "Construction and Demolition Operations—Safety and Health Program Requirements for Multi-Employer Work Projects."

American National Standards Institute. ANSI/CABO A117.1-1992, "Accessible and Usable Buildings and Facilities" (revision and redesignation of ANSI A117.1-1986).

EXECUTIVE SUMMARY — ELEMENT 12

Safety and health and environmental management have many similarities. They all focus on identifying and controlling hazards. Whereas safety and health management addresses hazards to people in the workplace, environmental management broadens the focus to people and other living things in the surrounding community and in other places affected by the organization's operations.

Environmental programs are often driven by regulatory compliance issues. Federal, state (or regional) and local governments in the United States, the European Union, Canada and Mexico have environmental regulatory requirements. In addition, there are numerous international environmental agreements in effect. Effective environmental management requires staying aware of, understanding and complying with these diverse, sometimes conflicting, requirements.

As with safety and health management, effective environmental management requires careful assessment of environmental hazards and their solutions followed by prioritization and action. This process involves evaluating all business operations for existing and potential adverse environmental effects and compliance issues, identifying solutions to eliminate or minimize the impact, and, where feasible, implementing them.

ENVIRONMENTAL MANAGEMENT

Environmental management addresses the impact of business operations on land, surface water (rivers, lakes, oceans), ground water and air. Pollution of these environmental elements can result in the exposure of people, plants and animals to harmful substances or energy sources. Most businesses, whether they produce services or products, have some adverse effect on the environment. Industrial operations may release hazardous substances from smokestacks, or possibly discharge pollutants into surface water or public treatment systems. Service industries may contribute to environmental problems by using tons of paper and other disposables that will end up in landfills, or by using and inappropriately disposing of hazardous chemicals, such as solvents, inks, and petroleum products. Failure of organizations to encourage use of mass transit options also contributes to air pollution.

The Environmental/Safety and Health Connection

Safety and health and environmental management have many similarities. Organizations often integrate the functions into a comprehensive safety, health and environmental management program. Both management areas are highly regulated technical disciplines that address exposure to hazardous agents: physical, chemical, biological or energy sources. In many companies, one department (or, in smaller organizations, one individual) serves as an internal consultant for safety, health and environmental regulations. Responsibility for program implementation rests with management.

Like other aspects of the safety and health program, environmental management needs the ongoing commitment and involvement of senior management to make sure environmental issues remain a priority. Senior management must understand that sound, proactive environmental management makes good business sense.

Compliance—the driving force

Most environmental efforts are driven by government regulations. Compliance with domestic and international laws provides a minimum standard for environmental management. In the United States, environmental laws are (generally) implemented by the U.S. Environmental Protection Agency (EPA) and by individual states. The regulations are based on laws to protect air, land and water resources. The major U.S. environmental laws are:

- Clean Air Act (and amendments) (CAA)

- Clean Water Act (and amendments) (CWA)

- Comprehensive Environmental Response, Compensation and Liability Act (CERCLA or Superfund, and amendments—The Superfund Amendments and Reauthorization Act [SARA])

- Emergency Response and Community Right-to-Know Act (SARA Title III)

- Hazardous Material Transportation Uniform Safety Act (HMTUSA)

- National Environmental Policy Act (NEPA)

- National Ocean Pollution Planning Act (NOPPA)

- Oil Pollution Act (OPA)

- Ports and Tanker Safety Act (PTSA)

- Radon Gas and Indoor Air Quality Research Act (RGIAQRA)

- Resource Conservation and Recovery Act (RCRA) (and amendments)

- Solid Waste Disposal Act (SWDA)

- Toxic Substances Control Act (TSCA)

- Used Oil Recycling Act (UORA)

These laws have spawned thousands of pages of regulations to implement and enforce their intent. Canada, Mexico and the European Union (EU) and its member states have strict environmental standards for facilities operating within their boundaries. Because the regulatory landscape is subject to change, it is best to check with the Environmental Protection Ministry or Department in the country of interest for current information on environmental regulatory issues.

International agreements addressing issues as diverse as mining rights, ocean dumping and the ozone layer also have been signed. These agreements often take several years beyond signing before they are implemented. However, they can have an impact on business operations even before full implementation. Examples of these international agreements are:

- The Antarctic Treaty (affects mineral exploration)
- Vienna Convention on the Protection of the Ozone Layer
- Convention on Long-Range Transboundary Air Pollution (controls nitrogen oxide and sulfur dioxide emissions in the United States and Europe)
- London Ocean Dumping Convention
- International Convention for the Prevention of Marine Pollution from Ships
- United National Environment Programme's Regional Seas Program
- 1982 United Nations Convention on the Law of the Sea
- 1973 Convention on International Trade in Endangered Species
- 1971 Ramsar Convention on Wetlands

Staying informed about the relevant and applicable U.S. (and state-level) and international regulatory standards is a critical activity of environmental management. Compliance requires understanding both the words and intent of the regulations. Environmental regulations can be extremely complex. In addition to routinely reading the *Federal Register* for proposed and new U.S. compliance standards and regulations, professionals who wish to stay informed should read trade and professional publications, as well as environmental regulation information service publications and newsletters, and should regularly attend seminars and workshops on regulations and compliance issues.

Although most environmental efforts are driven by compliance issues, in these environmentally aware times, organizations are also motivated by public perceptions. Potential negative publicity arising from an environmental incident or serious regulatory violation also motivates companies to strive for better environmental records. Going beyond compliance to take an environmentally proactive stance creates a positive image for an organization, potentially increasing its credibility and gaining trust for its products or services. Proactive companies often establish internal environmental standards for pollution prevention that go well beyond compliance. These companies take a leadership role in their industries, often providing a model for environmental excellence. Examples of such activity include establishing internal recycling and environmental awareness programs, and voluntarily researching and developing alternative, more environmentally responsible processes.

Beyond Compliance—Managing Environmental Risk

Effective environmental management goes beyond managing compliance to managing risk. Managing environmental risk involves identifying potential environmental threats posed by business operations and planning and executing a strategy to reduce or eliminate them. This systematic approach is process-oriented—that is, it requires examining procedures, processes and materials to find a better, more environmentally sound way to do the job. A systematic process of risk identification and reduction will often result in achieving regulatory goals and providing insight into future regulations. Trying to manage environmental issues solely through compliance management will result in a constant struggle to meet new and more stringent standards.

One of the most difficult parts of environmental management is coordinating the numerous and sometimes conflicting regulations applicable to a business. A risk assessment-based approach will focus on a process and enable the environmental professional to identify all applicable regulatory scenarios, needed permits and any apparent contradictions or conflicts.

The risk assessment approach begins with assessing management practices and all operations to identify:

- applicable regulations, including standards, required record keeping and permits (What are the requirements? Have they been met? What must be done to meet them? How much will it cost to comply? What will be the estimated costs of not complying? What are the other implications of compliance/noncompliance?)

- potential environmental threats, including those tied to specific regulations (Are any materials toxic or otherwise hazardous? Will the process release hazardous materials or substances into the air, water or land? How will the waste product be handled: recycling? land disposal? Could a hazardous material spill occur? How much hazardous waste does the process generate?)

- alternative materials and processes to accomplish the task in a more environmentally sound manner (Can a less hazardous raw material be used? Is there a way to make the process a closed loop so the waste stream is automatically reused and no waste is produced?)

Life cycle analyses and chemical stewardship use this approach to evaluate the environmental impact of materials, products and services from "cradle to grave"—from concept to end. In the manufacture of a product, this may be from raw materials through disposal of the finished product (and its by-products and packaging) at the end of its useful life. The analysis examines each phase of the product's life and considers the environmental impact of materials and processes for that phase. The analysis identifies the cause of the environmental impact and explores ways to minimize it by altering the process or materials. Services also have associated environmental impacts, and, like products, can undergo life cycle analysis.

Life cycle analysis is a systematic method of "designing in" sound environmental thinking (called "design for environment," or DFE). Other DFE approaches include pollution prevention, waste minimization, toxic use reduction and design for recycling. Design for recycling focuses on designing products for total recycling rather than disposal. One-use cameras, which are used up and returned to the photoprocessor, are an example of this concept. The film is removed and processed; the photographs are returned to the consumer and the camera to the manufacturer for re-use.

After conducting the assessments, companies need to prioritize environmental problems according to seriousness, potential for loss or environmental damage and potential regulatory implications, then plan and implement corrective measures in a systematic fashion. Quantifiable and realistic goals should be set based on the assessment and the priorities—e.g., reduce the amount of waste disposed of in landfills by 25% in six months. After the goals are set, responsible personnel should develop a strategy to reach the goals and evaluate progress. What steps are needed to reduce the landfilled waste? Is a recycling program feasible for office papers, corrugated cardboard or solvents? Can a process be redesigned as a "closed loop" so that waste material is automatically recirculated?

Whatever the design of the environmental program, it should be formal and in writing, and should clearly state guidelines and standards for the program and environmental performance. The formal program should also include procedures for achieving environmental performance standards along with a quantifiable way to measure performance.

Record keeping and documentation

The environmental management program should establish and maintain standards and procedures for keeping needed environmental records and other documentation.

Adequate records are essential for documenting the way in which hazardous materials are handled and compliance goals are met. In the United States, the EPA and state environmental agencies require comprehensive documentation concerning handling of hazardous wastes (from generation to disposal), air emissions, wastewater discharges, waste stream analyses and other environmental activities. Spills or other releases also must be accurately described and reported. Failure to maintain adequate records is a frequent cause of regulatory compliance violations.

Planning for emergencies

Organizations that use or produce a hazardous material or create hazardous by-products should have a contingency plan in case of a spill or other release. The contingency plan should identify the hazardous material, associated hazards, spill containment and cleanup procedures and emergency chain of command. Employees should be trained and prepared to respond to emergencies. Companies must be aware of reporting requirements of community right-to-know laws established by communities, states and national governments (in the United States or elsewhere).

Adequate technical support

Environmental management requires the expertise of numerous disciplines. Along with environmental and safety and health professionals, the environmental team may include in-house specialists from production, research/design and engineering, accounting, legal and purchasing functions. Outside resources also may be tapped: trade organizations can often provide technical assistance; consultants can fill gaps in in-house expertise.

Communication

Environmental issues are often emotional and controversial. Sometimes routine environmental problems become front-page news. Therefore, effective communication is a critical part of any environmental program. Effective communication must be ongoing, not initiated solely in response to a crisis. Communication should be viewed as a two-way street; it should provide opportunities for feedback. Communication channels must be maintained with local authorities; regulatory agencies at the state, local, federal and international levels; the public, associations, customers and suppliers and the media.

Employee involvement

Addressing environmental issues requires the involvement of everyone in the company. Maintenance, purchasing, production, distribution, research, administrative and other workers all affect environmental conditions through their work practices and attitudes. Environmental committees provide an excellent way for employees to become involved in the organization's environmental effort. All employees should feel comfortable alerting management to potential environmental problems. Effective solutions often originate with line workers.

Training

The success of any environmental program depends on training. Adequate and ongoing training will ensure that employees understand company policy and procedures and their individual roles in environmental improvement. Employee training should focus on awareness of corporate policy, roles and responsibilities, regulatory compliance and emergency response. All contractors must also be appropriately informed of the organization's environmental requirements.

Environmental Management Review

Like other aspects of the safety and health program, effective environmental management begins with the firm commitment of senior management. That commitment is established through a formal environmental policy, supported by adequate funding. Successful environmental programs are driven by a combination of regulatory compliance and the vision to move beyond simple compliance toward total risk management. The following worksheet will help you assess your organiza-

TABLE 12-1. ENVIRONMENTAL MANAGMENT REVIEW

| Issues/Questions | In Place | | | Action Plan |
	Yes	No	Partially	(if answer is "No" or "Partially")
12.1 Does the organization have an environmental policy that: ■ defines the scope of activities covered? ■ delineates lines of responsibility? ■ assigns accountability? ■ commits to provide environmental professionals with technical support? ■ delegates authority for establishing standards management intent? ■ establishes regulatory compliance as a minimum standard?				
12.2 Is there a formal, written environmental management program?				
12.3 Is adequate funding available for necessary environmental activities?				
12.4 Is management involved in the environmental program by reviewing data and providing feedback?				
12.5 Have the applicable environmental regulations and standards been identified and interpreted?				

TABLE 12-1. ENVIRONMENTAL MANAGEMENT REVIEW Continued

Issues/Questions	In Place Yes	No	Partially	Action Plan (if answer is "No" or "Partially")
12.6 Is the existing environmental program periodically reviewed?				
12.7 Are the required records kept? Are procedures in place to assure adequate record keeping?				
12.8 Have all needed permits been obtained?				
12.9 Is life cycle analysis performed to identify areas for improvement?				
12.10 Is compliance with performance standards monitored and reviewed on a regular basis? (Is the frequency adequate?)				
12.11 Is environmental data collected, analyzed and communicated?				
12.12 Are environmental assessments conducted? Are the results acted upon?				

tion's current environmental management program and plan for improvement.

References

Books

National Safety Council. *Accident Prevention Manual for Business & Industry: Administration & Programs,* 10th ed. Itasca, IL: NSC, 1992.

National Safety Council. *Accident Prevention Manual for Business & Industry: Environmental Issues.* Itasca, IL: NSC, 1995.

Articles

Dombrowski SLS. Chemical stewardship. *Plant Engineering,* April 23, 1992.

LaBar G. Is the environment right for voluntary protection? *Occupational Hazards,* October 1992.

Miner SG. Avoiding the big bang. *Occupational Hazards,* July 1990.

Miramon J, Stevens C. The trade/environment policy balance. *The OECD Observer* 176:25-27, 1992.

Pilko G. Beyond compliance. *Site Selection* 37(5):1015-1017, 1992.

Shapiro S. Global health, safety standards. *Business Insurance,* May 10, 1993.

Stickles RP, Firth LM. Facility risk management in developing countries. *Risk Management,* October 1990.

Packaged Training Program

National Safety Council. Agenda 2000® Safety Health Environment Program. Itasca, IL: NSC, 1992.

Government Publication

U.S. Environmental Protection Agency. *Waste Minimization Booklet.* Chicago: U.S. EPA-Region V, 1989. U.S. EPA has numerous booklets and brochures to help businesses comply with environmental regulations. Contact the nearest regional EPA office or state environmental agency for a complete list.

*E*XECUTIVE SUMMARY — *ELEMENT 13*

Work force planning and staffing begin with hiring and job placement. Companies can incorporate safety and health principles into their hiring and placement processes by specifying safety and health requirements, such as indicated in the job description and established by a Job Safety Analysis (JSA), and followed by administering physical examinations and health questionnaires. Many companies introduce basic safety and health concepts and procedures in their new-employee orientation programs, as well as provide specific information on required subjects such as hazard communication.

Safety and health work rules, or safe work requirements, are usually part of a company's safety and health program. Keys to the success of work rules include employee involvement in their development, effective communication and consistent enforcement.

Employee Assistance Programs (EAPs) are one way employers address personal problems that can affect an employee's ability to perform on the job. These programs can be an important part of a safety and health effort.

Under the Americans with Disabilities Act (ADA), employers are responsible for making reasonable accommodations for individuals with disabilites and ensuring that their workplace is accessible for individuals with disabilities. Because some organizations will have to make changes in job descriptions as well as workplaces, the act may have a large impact on work force planning and staffing.

WORK FORCE PLANNING AND STAFFING

An effective safety and health program addresses issues associated with work force planning, staffing and placement. Besides hiring and job placement, other important areas are safety and health work rules, employee assistance programs and requirements resulting from the Americans with Disabilities Act.

Hiring and Job Placement

Organizations traditionally try to hire the most qualified people they can, at a price they want to pay, to fill each position. While employees are expected to bring a set of skills to the workplace in exchange for wages and benefits, federal law requires that the employer provide a "safe and healthful place of employment, free from recognized hazards that cause or are likely to cause death or serious injury." Additionally, the employee is obligated by the same law to comply with all occupational safety and health standards, regulations and practices and procedures that apply to his or her own actions and conduct on the job.

In many companies, safety and health begins with writing job descriptions. In addition to spelling out the job's duties, a job description also specifies the employee's safety obligations, such as wearing personal protective equipment or observing no-smoking rules. A Job Safety Analysis (JSA) contributes to the formulation of a job description by establishing safety and health considerations related to the job (refer to Element 1 for more information on JSAs). Because safety needs can change with job responsibilities, companies need to write safety and health obligations in broad terms to eliminate the need to revise for any specific safety and health changes on the job. Responsible personnel should review the safety aspects of job descriptions with applicants to signal the company's commitment to safety even before hiring. For example, if employees must wear safety glasses on the job, that requirement should be pointed out and explained, so the applicant knows that wearing personal protective equipment is part of the job.

In addition to clearly stating job duties, some companies administer tests after a job offer has been made but before an applicant is hired, to screen applicants who do not meet documented requirements. For example, research has shown that applicants who are unable to meet the strength demands of their jobs suffer more injuries. Testing applicants for strength is acceptable *if* the strength requirements are quantified and are shown to be essential to accomplishing the job; at the same time, employers must make reasonable accommodations for disabled applicants. (See the section "Americans with Disabilities Act" in this chapter.)

Employers may administer tests and physical examinations only if they require them for all jobs in a particular category and if they can be clearly related to the job requirements. For example, a general strength test may be required for jobs that involve lifting. Because of their expense and low predictive value, many companies forgo some costly diagnostic tools, such as x rays to detect existing back injuries.

Some companies find that a good health questionnaire can be useful. It is important to note that medical inquiries, like tests, are allowed only after the job offer has been made but before the applicant is actually hired. Accurate data on injury/illness history can help employers match the capabilities of applicants with the demands of the workplace that can result in incidents and injuries.

To emphasize and reinforce desired performance, many organizations include safety and health on job performance evaluation forms. For example, a form might include questions about safe behavior, such as always wearing the proper protective equipment. The evaluations reflect the role of safety in performing job duties and reinforce safety requirements spelled out in job descriptions. Table 13-1 summarizes key hiring and placement tools.

TABLE 13 - 1: HIRING AND PLACEMENT TOOLS

Tool	Considerations
1. Job descriptions	Job descriptions must accurately reflect the physical and mental demands of the job.
2. Preplacement physical testing	Physical tests to measure skills and strengths required on the job must be required for all jobs in a particular category. Medical examinations must be conducted by qualified medical personnel.
3. Preplacement health questionnaire	The questions must be objective and asked of all emplyees. They must relate to the demands of the job and the actual workplace.

Safety orientation

The purpose of a safety orientation is to communicate the company's safety and health program components, activities, requirements and procedures. In addition, the orientation informs the employee of his or her safety and health responsibilities and the company's expectations.

Effective safety orientation includes three key features: company commitment, program comprehensiveness and specific job orientation on work assignments.

The company's *commitment* to safety is crucial if an employee is to accept the information presented in a safety orientation. Commitment is usually shown through subsequent statements and actions by management that reinforce the safety message. A representative from the human resources department often presents a general safety orientation through print and video materials; a portion of the session is sometimes conducted by a safety and health representative.

An effective safety and health orientation program should be comprehensive. It contains a basic orientation at the time of hire and job-specific training before the employee is allowed to work unsupervised on the job.

Different jobs present different hazards. The most effective training on a job's hazards and controls often comes from the immediate supervisor or a team leader who deals with the issues on a daily basis.

Age and gender

While companies may report varying rates of injuries and illnesses among employees of different ages or between men and women, they may not use the data when making hiring and placement decisions. However, the information may be useful after employees are on the job and the company is considering how to best train them. For example, both men and women can receive instruction in manual lifting. A traditional training program may need to be changed, however, to accommodate different needs of the two groups.

Safety and Health Work Rules

Safety and health work rules are specific requirements based on company policy and regulatory compliance. They are an integral part of a safety culture, which is the way safety is viewed in an organization. By posting rules, a company reminds its employees to follow basic safety and health requirements in their day-to-day work practices.

Characteristics of effective rules

Across all industries and job types, effective safety rules share several critical qualities. Good rules are:

Clearly stated.
To be easy to understand, rules should be in the simplest words, avoid technical jargon and be in active voice so employees know where different responsibilities lie. For example, "Wear hard hats on site at all times" or "Report all injuries, no matter how slight" are clearly stated work rules.

Positively phrased.
People respond better to positive wording; it is also usually clearer. For example, "Always wear rubber gloves on the job" is positive. "Don't work without rubber gloves" is negative.

Explained.
Short explanations avoid the impression of arbitrariness. For example, safe procedures always include one statement about good housekeeping. By explaining the problems that can be caused by disorder, the statement explains why neatness is important.

Fair.
Necessary rules are almost always perceived as fair by employees. Meaningless or unnecessarily restrictive rules and selective enforcement of rules can damage the credibility of all rules.

Limited in number.
Fewer rules indicate that managers realize that employees are adults and can exercise good judgment in most instances. The problem with long lists is that people can't remember all of them and so tend not to follow any of them.

Some examples of general safety rules are noted below.

- Follow instructions; don't take chances. If you don't know, ask before attempting the task.

- Report immediately any condition or practice you think might cause injury to employees or damage to equipment.

- Keep your work area neat and orderly. Put everything you use in its place.

- Use the right tools and equipment for the job and use them correctly.

- Get first aid promptly. Report incidents, injuries and illnesses immediately, regardless of how minor.

- Use, adjust, alter and repair equipment only when authorized.

- Wear personal protective equipment as directed. Keep it in good condition.

- Avoid disrupting others.

- Use the straight back leg lift for lifting. Get help for heavy or awkward loads.

- Obey all rules, signs and instructions.

Keys to success

Companies with effective safety work rules find that the keys to success lie in who develops the rules, how they are communicated and how they are enforced.

To develop safety work rules that are followed by all employees, include managers, labor representatives and experienced employees throughout the company in the process. This committee can be a special task force set up to create safety work rules, or the task can be addressed by an existing joint safety and health committee. In addition to increasing the likelihood that the procedures will address the needs of everyone in the company, a broad spectrum of members also ensures that employees will buy into the system. In some organizations, collective bargaining agreements incorporate safety and health as well as other safe work requirements.

Rules that are in place need to be communicated to everyone affected. Managers may use formal, written communications, such as safety manuals, but the effort must be more comprehensive and ongoing than a one-time effort. Good managers also provide crucial reinforcement for safety work rules by publishing related tips in a plant newsletter, displaying posters, providing pocket cards, etc., and including safety on the agenda at regular staff and department meetings. The informal communication network that exists in every organization can be equally powerful in transmitting safety rules to employees. Managers tap into this network by being good role models and by enforcing rules consistently.

Consistency is key to enforcing work rules. Employees may view safety work rules as a mechanism for assigning blame if they feel the rules are applied arbitrarily. A fair enforcement policy will include a system of applying and documenting increasingly severe disciplinary actions for employees who violate safety rules.

Employee Assistance Programs

Employee Assistance Programs (EAPs) are intended to help employees resolve alcohol, drug and other behavioral or stress-related problems that can interfere with an employee's ability to safely perform his or her job. In recent years, as health and fitness have become part of the corporate culture, EAPs also have begun offering such services as smoking cessation, exercise, weight control and nutrition counseling. Administration of EAPs varies throughout industry but is commonly placed within the purview of human resources management.

Americans with Disabilities Act (ADA)

Under the Americans with Disabilities Act, signed into law on July 26, 1990, one of the articles specifies that employers are responsible for providing a safe workplace for employees with disabilities. In addition, employers may not discriminate in employment against job applicants who have a physical or mental impairment that significantly limits or restricts "a major life activity." According to the President's Committee on Employment of People with Disabilities, such activities include hearing, seeing, speaking, walking, breathing and performing manual tasks.

Preparation

The law requires that employers analyze potential safety hazards prior to the placement of individuals with disabilities. All facilities must be accessible to individuals with disabilities who are being hired and placed in jobs. This includes the parking lot, entryways, common areas, restrooms and offices. Hazards need to be eliminated for all employees. Safety and health professionals need to be involved in designing reasonable accommodations for employees with disabilities.

Job Placement

The employee must be able, with the help of necessary accommodations, to handle the essential functions of the job. Job analyses will help identify the essential functions of a job and the required skills and abilities necessary to satisfactorily perform a job. When accommodations are needed, the facility or equipment must be modified to accommodate individuals with disabilities, except when this poses an undue hardship.

Working conditions that don't affect other employees may affect individuals with disabilities. For that reason, a study of working conditions for various jobs is essential when matching individuals with disabilities to appropriate jobs.

Accommodations

Employers can accommodate individuals with disabilities by:

- asking employees with disabilities for suggestions on types of accommodations
- identifying specific essential functions in job descriptions
- adjusting and redesigning equipment, when possible
- calling local rehabilitation professionals with experience in job accommodation

Accessibility

All areas of a facility must be made accessible to individuals with disabilities, including the parking lot and entryways; common areas such as the reception area, job application area, cafeteria and restrooms; and office and work areas.

Emergency Preparedness

The facility must have a plan and a procedure to notify all employees in case of an emergency and help them evacuate the facility. Rehabilitation professionals can help in developing an emergency preparedness program that considers the special needs of employees with disabilities. Emergency service agencies can assist in preparing evacuation plans.

Work Force Planning and Staffing Review

Review your company's existing work force planning and staffing policies from a safety and health perspective using the issues/questions in Table 13-2 as guidelines. Identify those items that are already in place; then, develop action plans for those not in place. The issues/questions are meant to be suggestions. You will no doubt have many issues/questions of your own to add.

TABLE 13 - 2. WORK FORCE PLANNING AND STAFFING REVIEW

Issues/Questions	In Place Yes	No	Partially	Action Plan (if answer is "No" or "Partially")
13.1 Do hiring and placement processes reflect a safety and health perspective?				
13.2 Is an effective safety and health orientation program in place for new employees?				
13.3 Are safety and health work rules in place? Are they clear, positive, fair and limited in number?				
13.4 Do safety and health work rules reflect input by a cross-section of employees, and are they communicated throughout the organization?				
13.5 Is an Employee Assistance Program in place?				
13.6 Is the organization in compliance with the Americans with Disabilities Act?				

References

Books

Bird FE, Germain GL. *Practical Loss Control Leadership*, 2nd ed. Loganville, GA: International Loss Control Institute, 1992.

National Safety Council. *Accident Prevention Manual for Business & Industry: Administration & Programs*, 10th ed. Itasca, IL: NSC, 1992.

Articles

Everly M. Are you ready for 1993? *Health & Safety at Work*, January 1993.

Government study sheds light on job safety differences between the United States and Mexico. *Workplace Safety & Health*, October 1992.

Hans M. Preemployment physicals and the ADA. *Safety & Health*, February 1992.

Harris JW. Crack down on safety violators. *Today's Supervisor*, April 1990.

Hatchette C. Use of accident histories in preemployment screening. *Risk Management*, January 1990.

Klubnik JP. Safety management: how to orient new employees. *Accident Prevention*, October 1987.

Magill MD. Setting the stage with a good orientation program. *Professional Safety*, February 1992.

Minter SG. Soft jobs? *Occupational Hazards*, October 1989.

Rogers M. Developing safety rules. *Accident Prevention*, August 1991.

Screening out unsafe workers—does it work? *Carpenter*, February 1983.

Smith B. Looking over the border. *Occupational Health & Safety* (England), December 1993.

Stones I, King W. Office overload. *Occupational Health & Safety Canada*, January 1991.

Vogel C. Fire can raze office buildings. *Safety & Health*, September 1991.

Packaged Training Program

National Safety Council. Agenda 2000® Safety Health Environment Program. Itasca, IL: NSC, 1992.

Government Publications

U.S. Department of Justice, U.S. Equal Employment Opportunity Commission. *Americans with Disabilities Act Handbook.* Pub. No. EEOC-BK-1. Washington, DC: U.S. GPO, 1991.

U.S. Department of Labor, Occupational Safety and Health Administration. Safety and Health Management Guidelines. *Federal Register,* vol. 54, no. 16. Washington, DC: U.S. GPO, January 26, 1989.

U.S. Equal Employment Opportunity Commission. *A Technical Assistance Manual on the Employment Provisions (Title I) of the Americans with Disabilities Act.* Pub. No. EEOC-M-1A. Washington, DC: U.S. GPO, 1991.

U.S. General Accounting Office. *Occupational Safety and Health: Differences Between Program in the United States and Canada.* GAO/HRD-94-15FS. Washington, DC: U.S. GAO, December 1993.

Guidebook

National Safety Council. *Guide to Americans with Disabilities Act.* Itasca, IL: NSC, 1992.

EXECUTIVE SUMMARY — ELEMENT 14

Knowing where and how specific safety policies and programs are succeeding or failing is crucial to continuous improvement. This chapter examines how to implement systems that can provide management with constant and meaningful data on the effectiveness of the safety and health program.

Thorough and objective evaluation of the overall safety and health program requires a variety of evaluation tools. The evaluation process must meet the discrete needs of each level of the organization. We examine the broad areas of concern at each level, as well as the types of assessments that address those concerns.

Self-assessment processes utilize trained internal staff to conduct inspections and other ongoing audits. Third-party processes employ consultants to execute comprehensive or complex assessments. Voluntary regulatory assessments involve the cooperative effort of the organization and a regulatory agency to improve safety and health in the workplace. We discuss the advantages and disadvantages of each method.

Any assessment process is incomplete until its findings have been reported to and acted upon by management in a timely and meaningful manner. Management must establish standards for assessment reports and procedures for follow-up that facilitate continuous improvement.

■ ■ ■ ■ ■ ■ ■ ■ ■ ■ ■ ■ ■

ASSESSMENTS, AUDITS AND EVALUATIONS

Throughout the world, regulatory agencies have worked for years to ensure that valid criteria exist for comparing individual safety and health programs to more universal standards. Local governments—states, provinces, even municipalities—can establish further criteria against which corporate programs must be measured. Yet, despite the proliferation of broad-based standards, truly meaningful evaluation of an organization's safety and health program remains a highly individualized process that must be thoughtfully structured by management.

This is not a simple task. Assessment instruments have been examined, refined and customized throughout the years of safety management's development as a discipline. As a result, we now have a wide—and sometimes bewildering—variety of instruments at our disposal. It is clear that no one audit or assessment tool can possibly serve every organization's needs; it is unlikely that a single instrument can even meet all the needs of one company. The task of management and safety professionals is to develop an assessment matrix—a series of instruments that, when used together, will accurately identify hazards and deficiencies as well as gauge the progress of corrective safety efforts.

An individual safety and health assessment tool may measure one or more of the following factors; an efficient combination of assessment instruments will measure all.

- Management effectiveness
- Compliance with standards
- Existing workplace hazards
- Behavior/safe job performance

It is a common tenet of management philosophy that "what gets measured gets done." For the purposes of our discussion, we would more aptly express this as "what gets measured gets targeted for improvement," because an effective assessment must be an educational tool. Assessments are not conducted merely to plot a succession of dots on a chart of the organization's safety and health progress; nor is it enough to merely list deficiencies. An assessment may involve an inspection process to discover hazards that are symptomatic of system failure, but its true intent is to lay the groundwork for remedy. The resulting report should educate the organizational level that has been evaluated as well as facilitating management's safety and health decisions.

To accomplish this end, we attempt to obtain objective results. Some instruments, such as perception surveys, measure subjective factors affecting the program; others, such as compliance audits, measure objective factors. Individual assessment processes may involve interviews, anonymous surveys, direct observation or site inspections. However, in every form and process, the goal is to obtain neutral results—factual statements, uncolored by bias or judgment, citing both strengths and weaknesses—that reflect what situations, behavior or attitudes currently exist. Such objectivity is a lofty goal for a human process; yet it is of such importance to meaningful evaluation that it will be reiterated throughout this chapter.

No assessment, or group of assessments, is an end in itself. The results of the overall assessment process should indicate to management the goals that must be achieved and the strategies that will likely achieve them; but those goals and strategies will themselves need to be periodically reevaluated, thereby molding the assessment process into a continuous improvement model.

Meeting the Assessment Needs of the Organization

Corporate and other select management groups need to know how the overall safety and health system is working, which is indicative of how effectively the program is being implemented. After an initial comprehensive assessment establishing a baseline, assessments of this scope are usually conducted every two to three years. The comprehensive assessment processes should concentrate on major trends and operations deficiencies that determine:

- five to ten key strategy recommendations with a scope of one to two years
- the subsequent matrix of assessments needed at the facility, operations and/or line levels

Management and operational groups at the facility or site level will need more detailed qualitative and quantitative data that focuses on site-specific managerial, technical and behavioral safety and health issues. Audits and assessments at the facility level are conducted for this purpose. Each facility should be audited as part of the scheduled comprehensive process that provides information for corporate and division strategic planning. However, at the site level, ongoing inspection processes and follow-up assessments concentrating on specific problem areas will play a larger role in continuous evaluation and improvement.

In small organizations, ongoing and problem-specific activities may even make up the bulk of the assessment process. Companies operating at one or two small sites—particularly service industries—may be able to identify program deficiencies through frequent, but less formal, inspections. However, management will still need to maintain its commitment by periodically evaluating the effectiveness and acceptance of its safety and health policies.

Taken as a whole, the corporate matrix of assessment instruments must meet the discrete needs of all organizational levels. The following is not intended as an in-depth review of specific assessment instruments; rather, it is a brief presentation of broad assessment types and how each can fit into the overall complex of assessments to meet the needs of various organizational levels. At the same time, our discussion will demonstrate how a variety of assessment types can complement one another to aid in thorough evaluations of all major areas of the safety and health program.

Management effectiveness: qualitative assessments

Managerial components of corporate, division and facility assessments will determine whether key management practices are in place to support the overall safety and health effort. Independent studies attempting to determine key management elements vary somewhat in detail; but generally the recommended "keys" are in accordance with the findings of a 1975 study conducted by the National Institute for Occupational Safety and Health (U.S.). This study found that effective safety and health programs (as measured by incident rates) have the following characteristics:

- Safety and health efforts receive high stature and commitment.

- Outside influences are used to instill safety-consciousness in the work force.

- A variety of promotional and recognition techniques are used.

- Both general and specialized job safety training is provided at the production level.

- Management takes a humanistic approach to the discipline of those who violate safety rules and policies.

- Frequent informal inspections are conducted to supplement formal audits.

- Both engineering and nonengineering approaches to incident prevention are used.

- The work force is stable.

The evaluation process may be part of a comprehensive audit of technical, managerial and performance/behavior issues conducted by an internal team (self-assessment) or by persons from outside the organization (third-party). The assessment process may involve:

- interviews with managers, supervisors and line employees

- documentation of management policies

- firsthand observation of management at work

In addition, the auditor may prepare and complete a formal audit instrument that examines management culture, practices and policies. The format of the instrument may range from a simple questionnaire to a more complex scored grid. Whatever the format, its purpose is to determine what management practices are in place to support safety and health programs and policies.

Candid self-assessment of management by management should also be part of the evaluation process. Certainly, in the incipient stages of any safety and health program, management should establish a baseline by identifying what practices are in place and what practices are needed to support the program. Goals are then reexamined and adjusted as the process is repeated in ensuing management assessments.

The worksheets included at the end of each chapter in this manual, used together, constitute a good template for a baseline self-assessment or review of management practices. Each set of worksheets will probably need to be refined to reflect your own company's culture, policies and programs. As the safety and health program matures, however, the questions posed in the self-evaluation process will not remain constant. Committed management should quickly progress beyond asking such questions as "Has a comprehensive series of baseline assessments been conducted at all organizational levels?" Once the answer to that question is "Yes," you will move on to determine, for example, whether strategic plans have been developed on the basis of baseline assessment results or whether a follow-up series of assessments has been scheduled at all organizational levels.

Safe job performance: Observations and samplings

Management will need to know if employees are adhering to established safety and health policies and procedures; therefore, they must determine what work practices are actually taking place at each site. In this area, assessment will be based on direct observation.

The observation-sampling system is rooted in the quality control principle of random inspections. In this case, the "inspection" is an observation of an employee at work. An observation form is developed using job safety analysis-based procedures and accident records. The observation form, listing specific standard practices, is then used during observations of employee job performance. Each task is scored either "safe" or "unsafe." Observers can then evaluate overall performance by calculating "safe" observations as a percentage of total observations (both safe and unsafe).

The observation-sampling system is by no means an assessment of the overall safety program; it is simply a direct and short-term measure of behavior. The observation-sampling method has also proved to be a good motivational tool for achieving positive short-term results (the correction of individual unsafe behavior) when followed up by supervisor-employee contacts. However, the primary value of this system to the assessment process is its directness. The information obtained through samplings can be used to interpret the validity of qualitative assessments; safe job performance is a reflection of management effectiveness.

We have simplified our explanation of the observation-sampling process and limited ourselves to a single sampling system. Setting up the measurement and validation systems will require training or the assistance of a statistician. Once the system is set up, however, sampling is a tool easily used by supervisors, mid-managers or safety professionals to accomplish ongoing evaluation of work practices.

Attitudes and acceptance: Perception surveys

Safety management systems and programs cannot be truly effective unless they are perceived as having value, and acted on accordingly, at all levels. Perception surveys express the subjective factors influencing the safety and health program—perceptions, attitudes, acceptance—in measurable terms.

Surveys identify programs and activities that employees feel lack relevance or management support and also pinpoint credibility gaps—the gaps between perceptions at various levels of the organization. Administered periodically, perception surveys can determine the effects of new safety and health initiatives, as well as overall improvement or deterioration of program effectiveness. All of this information helps to complete the picture sketched out by management's self-assessment process. Furthermore, survey results complement observation-sampling results by identifying employee attitudes that may be affecting safe job performance.

The assessment instrument itself is a questionnaire distributed to all levels of the organization. It is usually formulated, administered, analyzed and validated by a third-party firm. The vendor firm also generates an assessment report. This report interprets survey results that can be used to develop senior-level corporate strategies and mid-management performance objectives that target specific problem areas. Follow-up surveys are generally administered every one to three years, or when significant program or cultural changes have been implemented.

Self-Assessments

For our purposes, a self-assessment is defined as one that is conducted by individuals or groups from within the corporate structure. This can include professional staff or internal groups trained to conduct assessments.

Professional staff may come from the corporate, division or facility levels and may include safety professionals, occupational health professionals, risk managers or engineers. Internal groups may be safety committees, safety circles, operations teams or other task forces. Anyone within the corporate structure—managers, supervisors, line employees, labor representatives, maintenance and engineering personnel—can participate in the assessment process as long as he or she has been qualified to do so through specialized training.

The self-assessment plan should include a physical inspection of each facility. In the province of Ontario, Canada, for example, safety and health regulations require that specific worksite inspections be conducted each month, to cover the entire workplace at least once a year. The point is that everything—physical structures, maintenance systems, equipment, machinery, vehicles, emergency systems, etc.— should be inspected by someone, either staff or outside parties, on a regular basis. The scheduling of self-assessments or self-audits will be determined by the size and complexity of the facility. Very small sites can be inspected wall-to-wall in a single audit, while larger facilities may need to stagger the audit, conducting it in phases.

The purpose of self-assessments is to identify existing workplace hazards. However, an assessment should also determine whether operational-level personnel realize that procedures may need to be changed to accomplish safe job performance. This question is answered via documentation that demonstrates:

- where technical changes have occurred based on safety requirements

- design-in requirements, such as preoperation design reviews

- purchase requirements that place safety and health on an equal plane with cost, quality, efficiency and productivity

Self-assessment also is used to determine whether or not regulatory standards are being met in the workplace and to prepare the organization for compliance inspections conducted by regulatory agencies. Self-assessments/audits are sometimes limited in scope. However, they also may be conducted as part of an in-depth assessment of the overall safety and health program.

The expertise of those conducting self-assessments or self-audits can be crucial to the meaningful results of the evaluation. Specialized inspections (e.g., industrial hygiene surveys, compliance inspections) will require specific training, equipment and knowledge. This may well mean it is necessary to obtain the assistance of a qualified third party, particularly where professionals are not on staff.

Self-assessments that concentrated only on compliance issues were once the primary focus of safety and health assessments; however, as OSHA notes in its Voluntary Protection Program, it "has long recognized that compliance with its standards cannot by itself accomplish all the goals established by the [OSHAct of 1970]." Self-assessments remain important evaluation processes, but they are only one piece of the total assessment picture.

Since ongoing evaluation is key to continuous improvement, and because staff are more readily available than outside parties to participate in ongoing evaluation, self-assessments figure prominently in the overall corporate audit plan and schedule.

Maintaining objectivity

The issue of objectivity—obtaining neutral results—must be addressed when conducting self-assessments. Objectivity cannot be guaranteed in any assessment process, but it can be particularly difficult to maintain when those performing the assessment are members of the body being evaluated. Objectivity becomes the goal when deciding who will assess what.

One of the simplest means of promoting objectivity is to ensure distance between the evaluators and those being evaluated. In many organizations, facility assessment teams do not evaluate their own facilities; instead, they audit another facility's safety and health program. Corporate, division or facility professional staff can oversee the team's efforts and ensure that expertise is not lost in the transition from one site to another. Small, single-site organizations may need to take other measures to foster neutral results, such as including management, supervisors and employees on the assessment team so that diverse viewpoints are represented.

These are only suggestions. It is not our intent to outline how each organization can foster neutrality in the self-assessment process. The point is that, regardless of the size of the organization, management will need to plan for objectivity if self-assessment results are to be considered valid.

Training employees to conduct self-assessments

Management must also ensure that all staff participating in assessment processes are competent to execute their assignments and/or evaluate their findings. Third-party auditors, statisticians or surveyors come pretrained with credentials to validate their experience and areas of expertise. Internal personnel will need in-depth training to prepare for their role in self-assessment of the safety and health program; even staff professionals may not be familiar with all company operations and equipment or with every instrument to be used in the evaluation process.

Professionals experienced in the audit process should plan and conduct the training program for internal auditors. Training may also include accompanying a professional on several audits. Anyone charged with assessment responsibilities should become well versed in the following areas:

- Documentation procedures
- Creation of assessment reports
- Follow-up procedures

In addition, personnel should be competent in any skill or knowledge area applicable to the specific audit instrument. This may include interview skills (qualitative assessments), hazard identification and analysis and priority development (technical audits), knowledge of regulatory standards (compliance audits), statistical validation procedures (sampling), job safety analysis (observations) and so on.

Our list is necessarily incomplete because of the wide variety of instruments at management's disposal. We reiterate the point made in the discussion of objectivity: management will need to plan proficiency into the self-assessment program. This means that each chosen assessment tool must be carefully examined to determine what training is needed to ensure the tool is used properly.

Advantages of self-assessment: Continuity, control and involvement

If we heed the caveats associated with self-assessment (objectivity and expertise), we find that this method of evaluation has its advantages; principal among them is its contribution to a genuinely continuous improvement model. Third-party assessments cannot make up the bulk of an ongoing assessment methodology; internal staff are better placed and equipped for that responsibility.

Those conducting self-assessment should already have a working knowledge of the organization and the industry. They are familiar with corporate culture and operations, including equipment and materials involved; they know the basic functions and responsibilities of the various organizational levels, and are more likely to have a working knowledge of specific positions and jobs within the corporate framework. Moreover, staff become aware of organizational and procedural changes that affect the safety and health program as they occur. In short, internal assessment groups do not need to spend a great deal of time laying the groundwork for every assessment they conduct.

Management also retains more control over the assessment process when it is conducted internally. Third-party assessments usually occur in a single, uninterrupted process that moves methodically and comprehensively through the entire program or a broad problem area. Self-assessments, on the other hand, can be conducted in phases, covering the same ground as a third-party assessment, but with less disruption to normal operations.

Finally, self-assessment can be a means of augmenting the employee involvement program. Line employees must be trained before participating in assessment processes, but the training program alone will broaden employee safety awareness. Once employees are trained and begin to participate in evaluations, they are given a voice in the decision-making process; and the employee voice, based as it is on firsthand knowledge of operations and procedures, can actually facilitate the discovery of and solutions to problems in safety and health programs.

Third-Party Assessments

Third-party assessments are those performed by persons from outside the organization, including:

- representatives of regulatory agencies associated with consultation programs
- private-enterprise audit firms or individuals
- the National Safety Council

It should be noted that in large, geographically disbursed companies, assessments conducted by division or corporate personnel may be the equivalent of a third-party assessment in terms of objectivity, expertise and credibility.

Third parties are usually called upon to conduct:

- comprehensive assessments of the overall program

- in-depth assessments of specific technical/compliance problem areas

- special assessment processes (e.g., perception surveys) not easily handled by internal staff

- informal compliance audits (required or voluntary)

The frequency with which an individual organization will require third-party assessment services is a management decision. In small organizations—particularly in nontechnical industries (e.g., service industries)—the need for third-party assistance may well be minimal once staff have been thoroughly trained in the use of assessment tools. Large, complex and/or high-technology organizations may need to supplement ongoing evaluation processes with in-depth third-party assessments on a more frequent basis. Third-party perspective and expertise are of sufficient value that external evaluations should be scheduled into the overall assessment plan.

Selecting a third-party auditor

One of the primary advantages of third-party evaluation lies in the expertise of the persons conducting the assessment. The third-party individual or organization should be able and willing to verify experience through individual resumes and client references. Management, in consultation with staff professionals, can then make an educated selection that matches the assessment needs of the organization to appropriately qualified third parties. Candidates should possess the following qualifications:

- Familiarity with regulatory requirements

- Industry- and/or technology-specific experience/knowledge

- Audit/assessment experience

In the case of a compliance-based inspection, the auditor's knowledge of regulatory requirements is a prerequisite; in most other cases, management's selection of a third party is more fluid. While the technical or industrial background of an individual may be specified, a lack of experience with specific technology may be offset by broad experience within a given industry. Indeed, broad assessment experience with a variety of management models can be of greater value than specific technical knowledge in a comprehensive evaluation process.

Minimizing disruption: Preassessment and daily-findings reviews

Third-party assessments can be more disruptive to operations than internally conducted processes, particularly as they are likely to be more comprehensive and, therefore, more time-consuming. Management can smooth and expedite the third-party process by cooperating with the auditor's work, both before and during the assessment process.

The third-party auditor will need time to become familiar with organization-specific issues. Much of this can be accomplished by providing the auditor with background paperwork in the following areas several weeks before the auditor visits the facility:

- Management structure and culture

- Organization-specific safety and health policies, programs and procedures

- Materials and equipment involved in operations, including process flow diagrams for some types of assessments

- Loss history and statistical data

A preassessment review is then conducted, by telephone or in person, to clarify specific issues for the audit and to establish a logistical plan for the assessment process. The discussion of logistics should include:

- review of the negotiated scope and focus of the assessment

- scheduling for floor inspections and interviews

- establishing management, staff professional and floor contacts for the auditor

- scheduling the review of daily findings

- establishing the distribution of the assessment report

A daily review of assessment findings is advisable to further smooth the third-party process. The auditor presents findings or asks questions about issues that have arisen during the day, and internal staff have the opportunity to provide immediate feedback. These daily meetings provide information exchange and ensure that the assessment remains on track without unnecessarily diverging into side issues.

Advantages of third-party assessments: Objectivity, depth and credibility

Third-party evaluations are inherently more objective than internal processes. The external auditor is not biased by allegiance to the evaluated organization, nor motivated by organizational politics to color the assessment report in any fashion. Moreover, as an outsider, the auditor's perceptions have not become inured to the technical and cultural particulars of operations. By simple virtue of the fact that such items are not part of the external auditor's daily visual and mental landscape, he or she is less likely to miss details of facility inspections—housekeeping, maintenance, etc.—or the philosophical details of management policies.

Moreover, third-party auditors bring with them a universal viewpoint: their knowledge of what constitutes and supports a good safety and health program is based on experience and observation of a wide variety of organizational cultures and programs. This background—the aggregate audit experience—can be more valuable to thorough, accurate assessment than the auditor's expertise in any given area. A global perspective lends depth to third-party findings, reports and recommendations that even staff professionals may be unable to provide.

The effect of third-party objectivity and perspective is to render the assessment report more credible to many staff, from management to hourly employees. While this credibility may be partly a matter of perception, it can mean that valid assessment findings and recommendations are less threatening, and thus more readily accepted and acted upon, by those who have been evaluated. It is more difficult to dispute credible sources; just as quoted regulatory standards lend justification to citations of noncompliance, so the third party's expertise and objectivity lend authority to its assessment results.

We add one caution at this point. It is possible for less than scrupulous consultants to further their own interests by intimidating management into unnecessary follow-up consultations. While such conduct is uncommon, its possibility underlines the importance of obtaining and checking client references, requiring daily finding reviews and establishing standards for assessment reports.

Reporting and Follow-up

Assessment reports

The following guidelines for assessment reporting will hold true for all assessment reports. Regardless of what type of assessment is conducted, what specific techniques are used, or whether the assessment is conducted and reported on by internal or external groups, the audit or assessment report must always be an educational tool. The success or failure of the assessment—the ability of the evaluation system to effect meaningful change and continuous improvement—may well rest in the objectivity, expertise and completeness of the final report.

Each assessment process should conclude with a report to management. If the results are neutral and accurate, the report will detail both strengths and weaknesses in the safety and health program. Reported compliance deficiencies should cite the appropriate authority chapter and verse. Judgment calls based on the experience and expertise of the auditor should describe the physical hazard, unsafe work practices or other deficiency in specific terms—i.e., avoiding generalizations such as "unsafe work habits" in favor of specifics, such as "operator had removed the machine guard in order to increase production." Locations, machinery, etc., should also be specified and identified by their correct names.

Yet, the management report must go beyond the citation of assessment details— the results of interviews, observations, compliance deficiencies and/or identified hazards—and meld them into a cohesive overview of the program or problem area being evaluated. The auditor's report accomplishes this by analyzing the details to identify the generic root causes of similar hazards or deficiencies.

The report should encourage management to take corrective action quickly by including:

- a diagnosis of factors or situations that are causing problems
- a prognosis of when and where to expect trouble
- problems prioritized by likelihood of occurrence and loss potential
- guidelines for remedy, including alternatives and interim corrective measures

Once management has decided on a course of action, it then becomes the reporter, informing all affected individuals and organizational levels of its decisions and strategies. The report by management keeps all levels involved in the decision-making process by providing an opportunity for feedback.

Procedures should be established that specify when and to whom operating management submits its corrective action plan. Commonly, the report is required within 30 days and is distributed to mid-management and all persons who received the auditor's report. It is advisable to also include the auditor in the distribution, as he or she is in a position to offer constructive feedback regarding management's plan of action.

All formal reports become corporate records. Reports reinforce memory and provide a basis for comparing subsequent evaluations.

Follow-up

The management level that formulates the action plan must coordinate the follow-up. This will mean budgeting and scheduling for corrections, scheduling reinspections of physical hazards or noncompliance situations, and overseeing the efforts of those assigned specific responsibilities for corrective action.

The action plan should clearly assign responsibility, accountability and target dates for the correction of hazards and deficiencies uncovered in the assessment. Bear in mind that the action plan should cover the correction of isolated problems cited in the auditor's report and the generic problems—similar situations or behavior that could cause similar problems throughout the facility. Consequently, the action plan will very likely involve a range of corrective techniques—housekeeping, engineering, training, etc.—that will necessitate the participation of all levels and a variety of functions. Management should require complete reports from personnel accountable for follow-up to ensure that the action plan has been implemented.

Voluntary Regulatory Assessments

Organizations needing assistance in the identification and correction of hazards or the development of educational programs can contact OSHA for help. OSHA offers free comprehensive consultation services that involve appraisal of hazards, work practices, and/or corporate programs, assistance in the implementation of agency recommendations and follow-up inspections to ensure that required corrections have been made. These regulatory assessments are conducted by nonenforcement OSHA personnel. However, if the assessed organization fails to abate noted hazards that fall within OSHA's jurisdiction, the consultant will refer the matter for enforcement action.

Nonabatement and consequent enforcement referral is rare, since businesses that request assistance are usually committed to effective safety and health management. More often than not, the organization complies with cited OSHA requirements within the period allowed for hazard correction. Those businesses that request comprehensive evaluations, correct identified hazards and implement safety and health programs that meet OSHA's requirements are granted one-year exemption from programmed OSHA inspections.

Voluntary Protection Programs

OSHA's Voluntary Protection Programs (VPP) are designed to foster a cooperative relationship between management, labor and OSHA that promotes effective safety and health management. Approved VPP facilities have either designed and implemented safety and health programs that meet all OSHA criteria for effective safety and health management (Star Program); demonstrated potential and willingness to achieve Star status (Merit Program); or demonstrated alternative approaches to safety and health management that meet the purposes of Star criteria (Demonstration Program).

Interested organizations are asked to complete a concise self-assessment checklist as the initial step toward VPP participation. Once a formal application has been submitted and approved, nonenforcement OSHA personnel visit the site to conduct a document review, a facility walk-through and formal interviews. Those candidates that are finally approved for VPP are publicly designated as participants in the appropriate program category and removed from programmed inspection lists.

Our presentation of the VPP application process is greatly simplified. The criteria for participation are intentionally detailed and rigorous. The application itself involves paperwork and documentation that require a considerable commitment of staff time and effort. The OSHA assessment is thorough, and while citations are not issued, the site inspection can result in time-limited corrective "recommendations" for noted deficiencies. Successful applicants are exempted from programmed audits, but compliance remains mandatory, and VPP participants are periodically reassessed to confirm that they are maintaining VPP's high standards.

Yet, the sustained benefits of participation—improved morale and motivation, community recognition, program improvement and continued cooperative assistance from OSHA—can far outweigh the temporary disadvantages; and involvement in VPP, or similar voluntary programs, should be duly considered by management. At the very least, the internal and external assessments involved in the application process can contribute significantly to program evaluation; successful application can signal the achievement of a new milestone in the continuous improvement of safety and health management.

Assessments, Audits and Evaluations Review

The following review suggests some of the questions management must answer in order to evaluate its organization's assessment/audit program and to begin to establish the baseline status of current assessment systems. This review is a guideline; as you work through it, you will want to consider assessment issues specific to your company's needs, culture, and structure.

TABLE 14 - 1. ASSESSMENTS, AUDITS AND EVALUATIONS REVIEW

Issues/Questions	In Place Yes	No	Partially	Action Plan (if answer is "No" or "Partially")
14.1 Are a variety of assessment tools used in the company assessment program?				
14.2 Has a comprehensive baseline series of assessments been conducted at all organizational levels?				
14.3 Does senior management regularly assess its safety and health strategies and goals? Are these self-assessments compared to other assessment results?				
14.4 Are assessments conducted at all company levels—corporate, division and facility?				

TABLE 14 - 1. ASSESSMENTS, AUDITS AND EVALUATIONS REVIEW Continued

| Issues/Questions | In Place | | | Action Plan |
	Yes	No	Partially	(if answer is "No" or "Partially")
14.5 Does the overall assessment system include both internal and external assessment processes?				
14.6 Are internal audit staff trained by professionals? Have they accompanied a professional on an audit?				
14.7 Are credentials and client references required of third-party auditors?				
14.8 Do third-party audits include preassessment and daily findings reviews?				
14.9 Are standards and procedures established for assessment reporting and follow-up?				

TABLE 14 - 1. ASSESSMENTS, AUDITS AND EVALUATIONS REVIEW Continued

Issues/Questions	In Place Yes	No	Partially	Action Plan (if answer is "No" or "Partially")
14.10 Does the organization conduct voluntary regulatory assessments?				
14.11 Does the assessment program evaluate all of the following: management effectiveness, compliance with standards, existing hazards, safe job performance?				

References

Books

Kase D, Wiese K. *Safety Auditing: A Management Tool.* New York: Van Nostrand Reinhold, 1990.

LaDou J, ed. *Occupational Health & Safety,* 2nd ed. Itasca, IL: National Safety Council, 1994.

Manuele F. *On the Practice of Safety.* New York: Van Nostrand Reinhold, 1993.

National Safety Council. *Accident Prevention Manual for Business and Industry: Administration & Programs,* 10th ed. Itasca, IL: NSC, 1992.

Articles

Bailey CW. Improve safety program perception. *Professional Safety,* October 1993.

Bailey CW, Petersen D. Using perception surveys to assess safety system effectiveness. *Professional Safety,* February 1989.

Flatlow S. OSHA's voluntary program can yield cost benefits. *Transport Topics,* July 19, 1993.

Packaged Training Programs

Kaletta JP. Burlington Northern Railroad Executive Leadership Series. Itasca, IL: National Safety Council, 1993.

National Safety Council. Agenda 2000® Safety Health Environment Program. Itasca, IL: NSC, 1992.

Petersen D. The Dan Petersen Safety Management Series. Safety Training Systems, 1990.

Government Publications

Cohen A, Smith M, et al. *Safety Program Practices in High Versus Low Accident Rate Companies*. Washington, DC: U.S. Department of Health, Education, and Welfare, 1975.

Occupational Safety and Health Administration, Voluntary Protection Programs. *Federal Register,* vol. 53, no. 133. Washington, DC: U.S. GPO, July 12, 1988.

Report

Industrial Accident Prevention Association. Developing Your Health & Safety Policy and Program: A Guide for Employers. Ontario, Canada: IAPA, March 1992.

APPENDIX
Resources for Safety, Health and Environmental Standards and Policies

Global

International Labour Office (ILO)
International Occupational Safety and Health
Information Centre (CIS)
    4, rue des Morillons
    CH-1211 Geneva 22
    Switzerland

Africa — Regional Adviser Working Conditions
    ILO Office Dar Es Salaam
    POB 9212
    Dar Es Salaam
    Tanzania

Latin-American Centre for Occupational Safety
and Health
    Rua Capote Valente 710
    Pinheiros
    CEP 05409
    Sao Paulo, SP
    Brazil

ILO Regional Office for Asia and the Pacific
    P.O. Box 1759
    Bangkok
    Thailand

International Social Security Association (ISSA)
    17/19 place de l'Argonne
    F-75019 Paris
    France

International Standards Organization (ISO)
    1, rue de Varembe
    Case Postale 56
    CH-1121 Geneva 20
    Switzerland

World Health Organization (WHO)
    CH-1211
    Geneva 27
    Switzerland

America

Canada
Natural Resources Canada
    580 Booth Street
    Ottawa, Ontario K1A OE4

Labour Canada
    Occupational Safety and Health Branch
    (OSHB)
    Ottawa, Ontario K1A OJ2

Latin America
(See ILO Regional Adviser under Global)

Mexico
Mexican Secretariat of Labour and
Social Welfare
    Anillo Periferico Sur Blvd. Adolfo Ruiz
    Cortines 4271
    Edificio A, Nivel 9
    Col. Fuented Del Pedregal
    14149 Mexico, D.F.

United States of America
American National Standards Institute
    11 West 42nd Street
    New York, NY 10036

Consumer Product Safety Commission
    4330 East West Highway
    Bethesda, MD 20814-4408

Energy Department
    1000 Independence Avenue S.W.
    Washington, DC 20585

Environmental Protection Agency
    401 M Street S.W.
    Washington, DC 20460

Mine Safety and Health Administration
    4015 Wilson Boulevard, Room 601
    Arlington, VA 22203

National Fire Protection Association
    Batterymarch Park
    Quincy, MA 02269

National Institute for Occupational Safety
and Health
Centers for Disease Control
Publications Division
Robert Taft Building
4676 Columbia Parkway, Mailstop C13
Cincinnati, OH 45226

National Safety Council
1121 Spring Lake Drive
Itasca, IL 60143-3201

Department of Labor, OSHA
200 Constitution Avenue N.W.
Washington, DC 20210

U.S. Department of Transportation
400 7th Street S.W.
Washington, DC 20590

Asia

China
Ministry of Labour, Inspectorate of
Occupational Safety and Health
12 Hepinglizhong Jie
Dongcheng Qu
Beijing

India
Ministry of Labour
Shram Shakti Bhawan
Rafi Marg
New Delhi 110 001

Japan
Ministry of Labour
2-2 Kasumigaseki
1-chome
Chiyoda-ku
Tokyo

Environmental Agency
1-2-2 Kasumigaseki
Chiyoda-ku
Tokyo

Malaysia
Ministry of Labour
Tingkat 1-3 (Level 2-4)
Pusat Bandar Damansara
50530 Kuala Lumpur

Saudi Arabia
Ministry of Labour and Social Affairs
Riyadh 11157

Thailand
Department of Labour
Asdang Road
Bangkok 10200

Europe

European Community
Commission of the European Communities
Directorate General XI
Environmental, Consumer Protection and
Nuclear Safety
200 rue de la Loi
B-1049 Brussels
Belgium

Economic and Social Committee
2 rue Ravenstein
B-1050 Brussels
Belgium

European Committee for Standardization
(CEN)
36 rue de Stassart
B-1050 Brussels
Belgium

Institute for European Environmental Policy
3 Endsleigh St.
London
WC1H 0DD
England

France
Ministry of Labour, Employment and
Professional Training
127 rue de Grenelle
75700 Paris

Germany

Federal Ministry of Labour and Social Affairs
    5300 Bonn 1
    Rochusstrasse 1
    Postfach 140280

Federal Institute for Occupational Safety
and Health
    Vogelpothsweg 50-52
    4600 Dortmund 1

Ministry of the Environment
    5300 Bonn 2
    Kennedyallee 5

Great Britain

Health and Safety Executive
    Library and Information Services
    Broad Lane
    Sheffield S3 7HQ

Department of the Environment
    2 Marsham Street
    London, SW1P 3EB

Greece

Ministry of the Environment, Physical Planning
and Public Works
    Odos Amaliados 17
    115 23 Athens

Ministry of Labour
    Odos Pireos 40
    Athens

Ireland

Department of the Environment
    Custom House
    Dublin 1

Labour Department
    Davitt House
    Mespil Road
    Dublin 4

Italy

Ministry of the Environment
    Piazza Venezia 11
    00187 Rome

Ministry of Employment and Social Welfare
    Via Flavia 6
    00187 Rome

Luxembourg

Ministry of the Environment
    18 montee de la Petrusse
    2918 Luxembourg

Ministry of Labour
    26 rue Zithe
    2939 Luxembourg

Netherlands

Ministry of Housing, Physical Planning and
the Environment
    Van Alkemadelaan 85
    2597 AC
    The Hague

Ministry of Social Affairs and Employment
    Anna van Hannoverstraat 4
    POB 90801
    2509 LV
    The Hague

Portugal

Directorate General of Occupational Safety
and Health
    Av. da Republica, 84-5
    1600 Lisbon

Ministry of the Environment and
Natural Resources
    Av. D. Carlos I 126-6°
    1200 Lisbon

Spain

Ministry of Labour and Social Security
    Agustin de Bethancourt 4
    28003 Madrid

Note: This is a limited directory of available resources. Additional information can be obtained from governmental agencies and departments of state and commerce.

INDEX